Into Full Flower

It is a delight to eavesdrop, as it were, on the conversation between Elise Boulding, a friend and colleague for fifty-five years, and Daisaku Ikeda, whom I know only through his words—two visionary thinkers and unabashed humanists. Coming from different traditions, they share a profound commitment to peace and human welfare, to diversity and world citizenship, to open listening and dialogue, and to envisioning and building a better future. In a flowing dialogue, they build on each other's experiences and ideas to produce valuable insights for creating peace cultures.

—Herbert Kelman, Richard Clarke Cabot Professor
of Social Ethics, Emeritus, Harvard University

This animated conversation between Elise Boulding and Daisaku Ikeda covers many intriguing topics in the field of peace culture. Each draws upon decades of personal experience, and their dialogue winds its way from the small-scale but crucial details of family life, through the organization and practice of education, to the broad lessons of intercultural learning. Boulding and Ikeda encourage us to rethink our own priorities and to consider alternatives that are more social, peaceful, just, and fun.

—Paul Joseph, Professor of Sociology, and Director,
Peace and Justice Studies Program, Tufts University

This book is a wonderful encapsulation of so much of what is important and necessary to transform our present global war culture into one of peace, sustainability, and hope. In this series of dialogues, Daisaku Ikeda and Elise Boulding share with readers their rich wisdom, based on their lifetimes of studying, speaking, and writing of the importance of a sea change in our values. The authors point out that we must learn to move from an ethos of individualism to one of conversation, caring and compassion, as we seek, without enmity, to understand one another across the differences that divide us. Education must be at the forefront of such movements for building peace. This kind of education honors the creative spirit and energy of each individual, yet calls us, at the same time, into community. True peace and happiness begins with each of us as individuals, yet can only be fulfilled when each of us works conjointly for the happiness of others as much as for ourselves. It is in the constant connections with members of our human family that the true basis of peace lies. Good pedagogy is connected to a reverence for life and is rooted in life's most diverse experiences.

Ikeda and Boulding point out that changing our culture cannot happen without honoring the contributions of women and without giving credence to the traditional feminine values of nurturing, listening, and caring. Social reform and any building of peace culture must rest both upon the firm foundation of the inner transformative work of the human heart and upon an ethos of love.

—Mary Lee Morrison, Founding Director of Pax Educare, Inc., and author of *Elise Boulding: A Life in the Cause of Peace*

Into Full Flower

Into Full Flower

Making Peace Cultures Happen

ELISE BOULDING
DAISAKU IKEDA

Dialogue Path Press
Cambridge, Massachusetts
2010

Published by Dialogue Path Press
Ikeda Center for Peace, Learning, and Dialogue
396 Harvard Street
Cambridge, Massachusetts 02138

Appendix One is published by permission of *CrossCurrents* magazine

Cover design by Schwadesign
Interior design by Eric Edstam

This book originally appeared in Japanese under the title *Heiwa no bunka no kagayaku seiki e* (Building a Century of Peace Cultures), published by Ushio Publishers, Tokyo, 2006.

ISBN: 978-1-887917-08-7

Library of Congress Cataloging-in-Publication Data

Boulding, Elise.
  [Heiwa no bunka no kagayaku seiki e. English]
  Into full flower : making peace cultures happen / Elise Boulding, Daisaku Ikeda.
    p. cm.
  Includes bibliographical references and index.
  ISBN 978-1-887917-08-7 (pbk. : alk. paper)
1. Peace-building. 2. Boulding, Elise—Interviews. 3. Ikeda, Daisaku—Interviews.
I. Ikeda, Daisaku. II. Title.
  JZ5538.B68513 2010
  303.6'6—dc22

                                              2010001407

10 9 8 7 6 5 4 3 2

About the Ikeda Center

The Ikeda Center for Peace, Learning, and Dialogue is a nonprofit institute founded by Buddhist thinker and leader Daisaku Ikeda in 1993. Located in Cambridge, Massachusetts, the Center engages diverse scholars, activists, and social innovators in the search for the ideas and solutions that will assist in the peaceful evolution of humanity. Ikeda Center programs include public forums and scholarly seminars that are organized collaboratively and offer a range of perspectives on key issues in global ethics. The Center was originally called the Boston Research Center for the 21st Century and became the Ikeda Center in 2009.

Dialogue Path Press is the publishing arm of the Center and is dedicated to publishing titles that will foster cross-cultural dialogue and greater human flourishing in the years to come. Prior to the founding of Dialogue Path Press, the Center developed and published books in collaboration with publishers such as Orbis Books, Teachers College Press, and Wisdom Publications. These books, which focus on topics in education and global ethics, have been used in more than 650 college and university courses to date (2010). *Into Full Flower: Making Peace Cultures Happen* is the second title to be published by Dialogue Path Press, following *Creating Waldens: An East-West Conversation on the American Renaissance* in 2009.

For more information, visit the Ikeda Center Web site: www.ikedacenter.org

Contents

Foreword

It is with great joy that I commend this book, *Into Full Flower: Making Peace Cultures Happen*, to the widest possible readership. The two brilliant minds of Elise Boulding and Daisaku Ikeda share their wisdom across cultures, spanning the twentieth and twenty-first centuries. Their intellectual contributions have been guided by open hearts and deep faith in the potential of our human family to evolve toward greater planetary awareness and responsibility.

Both these great souls have been teachers and mentors for me—inspiring my faith in the life force and its wondrous unfolding on our home planet, earth. Both see our twenty-first century as the century of women, as women take their place in all societies, equal partners at every level of decision-making.

This book is timely as well as timeless in its rich discussions of the importance of education and respecting all human cultures. In the United States, President Barack Obama echoes similar views and reengages with the United Nations in a renewed commitment to inclusive global agreements to solve today's crises in finance, climate, poverty, pollution, disease, ignorance, and inequality. Clearly, as Dr. Boulding and Mr. Ikeda remind us, cooperation and mutual understanding provide the only way forward in our interdependent world.

I remember, long before I met her, how electrified I was reading Dr. Boulding's groundbreaking book *The Underside of History: A View of Women through Time* (1976), which corrected so many misperceptions and documented the crucial contributions of women through the ages and in every field from art to science, from literature to service in families and communities.

This book was followed in 1977 by *Women in the Twentieth Century World*, in which Dr. Boulding presented the statistics and documentation of women's indispensable work in the world and encouraged us all to build on our achievements. I am still thrilled as I read her personal inscriptions to me in these two books.

Her magnum opus, *Cultures of Peace: The Hidden Side of History* (2000), presaged the new focus of the United Nations and many world leaders on the vital role of women in all negotiations to end conflicts and wars, and to lay down pragmatic conditions for peace. As women now become even more prominent in business, finance, and entrepreneurship, we are all standing on Dr. Boulding's shoulders.

I was also honored to know Dr. Boulding's husband, the famous economist Kenneth Boulding, who encouraged me in many ways as I challenged the obsolete orthodoxies of economic textbooks and the destruction they wrought in many countries, widening poverty and inequality while despoiling the environment—our collective life-support system on this planet. In 1996, Elise Boulding wrote the foreword to the new edition of my 1978 book, *Creating Alternative Futures: The End of Economics*, calling me her "favorite paradigm smasher"! Both

Bouldings and their exemplary marriage and partnership were great inspirations.

I was equally fortunate to connect with Mr. Ikeda through the efforts of Masao Yokota of the Soka Gakkai International, who tirelessly shuttled between Boston and Tokyo, helping to build the Boston Research Center for the 21st Century with Virginia Benson. It is fitting that this Center is now renamed to honor Mr. Ikeda, its founder, as the Ikeda Center for Peace, Learning, and Dialogue. I remember my surprise and joy to be honored with the Center's Global Citizen Award, shared with Nobel Peace Prize laureate Adolfo Pérez Esquivel in 1996.

During several trips to Tokyo, I met many times with Mr. Ikeda and Kaneko Ikeda, his wife in their exemplary partnership over the years. I shall always cherish my dialogue with Mr. Ikeda, published in 2004 as *Planetary Citizenship*, and the process by which it was facilitated over many months by Mr. Yokota, who couriered the audiotapes and transcripts back and forth between my home in Florida and Mr. Ikeda in Tokyo.

Mr. Ikeda's passion for peace and intercultural dialogue has provided the inspiration and basis for his extraordinary series of books with great writers, thinkers, and political leaders. His dialogue with Arnold Toynbee, *Choose Life* (1976), is particularly meaningful to me as a British-born writer. Mr. Ikeda tells the story of Toynbee's bravery in challenging the racism and xenophobia in Britain against the Turks.

Mr. Ikeda's dialogues with Aurelio Peccei (*Before It Is Too Late*, 1984) and Norman Cousins, who were also my friends and mentors, are very meaningful to me. I learned much from his dialogue with Mikhail Gorbachev (*Moral Lessons of the Twentieth Century*, 1996), whom I honor and am fortunate to have come to know personally.

Mr. Ikeda's constant work on peace and the abolition of nuclear weapons led to his annual peace proposals to the United

Nations. At last, his efforts bore fruit in the Security Council Resolution on eliminating nuclear weapons in September 2009. Mr. Ikeda's dialogues with Dr. Johan Galtung (*Choose Peace*, 1995) and David Krieger (*Choose Hope*, 2001) have been equally influential, as were his meetings in China with Zhou Enlai and many other Asian leaders.

One by One (2004) is an inspiring compilation of stories by Mr. Ikeda about writers, poets, and leaders from all walks of life and around the world, from Chinese painter Fang Zhaoling and Mahatma Gandhi to civil rights leader Rosa Parks and Valentina Tereshkova, the first woman in space. *One by One* includes the DVD of a wonderful film, *Another Way of Seeing Things*, which can be viewed at www.EthicalMarkets.tv, the video site I created to help reform markets and grow the green economy globally.

Dr. Boulding and Mr. Ikeda are truly timeless leaders, for they reach into the heart of the human experience with love and humility. A special joy for me in introducing this book is that they share with me a love of poetry and faith in the potential of all in our human family.

Hazel Henderson
September 2009

CONVERSATION ONE

Peace in the Family

CIRCLES OF CONVERSATION

IKEDA: I am honored to have this opportunity for dialogue with you, Dr. Boulding. A great scholar and activist, you have devoted your entire life to the cause of peace.

BOULDING: I, too, am grateful for the chance. Dialogues in which people heed the inner voices of human spirituality are of the greatest importance. I know well how energetically you work for world peace as president of the Soka Gakkai International. In these times of deepening confusion, I, too, work for peace and joy in the world and should like to join you in seeking ways to make them possible.

IKEDA: You do me a great honor. We will be conducting our dialogue primarily through correspondence. One important aim is to transmit your frankly expressed philosophy and pacifist message to people all over the world.

BOULDING: Thank you.

IKEDA: Over many years, you have maintained a relationship with the Soka Gakkai women's division, supporting and showing profound understanding of their peace and cultural activities. You consulted on the exhibition titled "Women and the Culture of Peace," organized by the Soka Gakkai Women's Peace Committee and the Young Women's Conference on Peace and Culture. Owing to your assistance, the exhibition, which first opened in June 2002, garnered tremendous interest throughout Japan. As of this point (in 2005), some 420,000 people in nine cities have viewed it.[1] Your message in the exhibition to "Be peacemakers!" has made a deep impression on many women.

BOULDING: I am delighted the exhibition has been a success. I take immense pleasure in being useful to women's grassroots movements.

IKEDA: I believe you met with some Soka Gakkai women during a 1984 stay in Japan.

BOULDING: Yes, I was perfectly at home with them. I remember their animated exchanges as they sat talking in a circle.

IKEDA: In the SGI, we stress small meetings, called discussion meetings, based on openhearted, cheerful, and supportive dialogue.

BOULDING: The discussion meeting represents a very rational approach. Peace groups, too, usually sit informally in circles where people can see one another's faces in total equality, hear everything that is said, get to know one another better, and deal more effectively with project agendas. Because it has these advantages, the so-called listening circle is becoming popular internationally.

IKEDA: For years, you combined your efforts toward world peace with your responsibilities as a wife, homemaker, and mother of five children. Through your work at the United Nations Educational, Scientific, and Cultural Organization (UNESCO) and the United Nations University, and as a professor of sociology and peace studies at several American universities, you have spread peace culture. Thank you as well for supporting the Boston Research Center for the 21st Century (renamed the Ikeda Center for Peace, Learning, and Dialogue in 2009) and the Toda Institute for Global Peace and Policy Research, both of which I founded (in 1993 and 1996, respectively).

BOULDING: Not at all. SGI members and I share the same ideas on peace. We are partners.

To Learn From One Another

IKEDA: Your late husband, Kenneth Boulding, was a great economist and peace researcher. The two of you were a famously devoted couple working hand in hand for peace.

Employing the striking image of "spaceship earth," your husband outlined how we ought to live in a global age. The year before he died, I received a copy of his book *Towards a New Economics: Critical Essays on Ecology, Distribution, and Other Themes* (1992), which I still treasure. His beliefs are condensed in the book's dedication, "For Peace."

In a 1992 interview in the *Seikyo Shimbun*, the Soka Gakkai newspaper, you shared your thoughts on one of my annual peace proposals.[2] Thank you again.

BOULDING: Kenneth thought very highly of your peace proposals. Even after living together for fifty years, he and I sometimes thought differently. He was an economist, and I am a sociologist. But we agreed in our sympathy with the SGI movement.

IKEDA: We are grateful for that and for the work you and Kenneth did in helping to build the peace studies movement in Japan. In your husband's later years, you worked together to counsel students at the University of Colorado. I am interested in learning what inspired the two of you to devote yourselves to peace research, activism, and education. But first, please tell me how you first met Kenneth and how your pacifist convictions brought you together.

BOULDING: I remember it as if it were yesterday. Ours was a very romantic story. A few months after I graduated from the New Jersey College of Women, now Douglass College, I decided to become a Quaker. And at the very first Quaker worship meeting I attended, I met Kenneth. We understood each other at once because we were both committed to peacemaking.

He proposed eighteen days later. I was taken aback. He was thirty-one, and I was twenty-one. He was ready for marriage, but I was just out of college. Although very much in love, I thought we needed more preparation time. Nonetheless, planning went ahead, and we had a Quaker wedding in August 1941.

How did you and your wife come to meet?

IKEDA: I met my wife, Kaneko, through Soka Gakkai activities. We married when she was twenty and I was twenty-four.

Although we were poor and unknown, our life was happy and fulfilled.

Our mentor, Josei Toda, the second president of the Soka Gakkai, watched over us warmly. We vowed that, instead of living selfishly, we would encourage each other to overcome all hardships in building a world of happiness for everyone.

BOULDING: Kenneth and I talked seriously about our family: how we would raise our children to be peacemakers and how we could contribute to the world we lived in.

IKEDA: Your goal to raise children to be peacemakers reveals the depth of your passion for peace. Where were you living then?

BOULDING: Because Kenneth was going to work for the League of Nations, we moved to Princeton, New Jersey, where, because of World War I, the economic and financial section of the League had relocated from Geneva, Switzerland. We wanted children, but it took me five years to get pregnant. During those years, I spent my time learning everything I could from my husband. We were partners, but he was also my teacher.

IKEDA: To respect and learn from each other is the ideal for a couple. I was wondering what things you emphasized most in raising your five children.

BOULDING: Our Quaker faith was basic to our family life. Daily family quiet time was very important.

IKEDA: When it comes to matters of faith, I have always believed in the importance of prayer. It gives us a chance to self-reflect while discovering and developing our capacity for caring.

It also leads us to ponder the phenomena of the universe and our interdependence with the universe. Prayer, to me, is the essence of religion. Without prayer, there can be no self-improvement.

BOULDING: Of course, family life was not all quiet time or prayer. There were always practical matters to decide. Just as Quakers make decisions at group business meetings, so we held a family business meeting every few weeks to do things like allotting domestic chores. In the evenings, we often had family readings from books Kenneth and I loved. When the children were small, I spent a few minutes with each at bedtime.

IKEDA: Wonderful! The Soka Gakkai women have led a Japan-wide movement to encourage reading aloud to children. Many mothers happily report that their children have come to love books and are now better behaved as a result.

BOULDING: Going to hear their father address conferences was another activity the children shared. Long before our marriage, Kenneth was already much in demand as a public speaker. We always had a car big enough for all the children to pile into so we could go with him to conferences whenever possible.

Start With the Local

IKEDA: The family and local community surely are critical in bringing peace culture to full flower.

BOULDING: Yes, without peace building in the family and local community, even organizations like the United Nations cannot succeed. That is why I always made a point of getting to know my neighbors: We must know one another to help one another. Peace is not only about acting in times of danger, it is also about assisting one another in daily life. The family and local community are key starting points.

IKEDA: In the SGI, we also place great emphasis on our local communities. Determined to be good citizens of our communities, we promote a popular movement of peace, culture, and education. We believe in the paramount importance of steadily forming ties of friendship in our communities and offering wholehearted encouragement to those who are suffering. Any movement that tries to work separate from the community can never gain its support.

We must forever remember that, as the basic social unit, the family is of utmost importance. Your research is unique in looking at peace from a mother's perspective. You have stressed both the family unit and the mission of women in fostering peace culture.

BOULDING: Well, yes. But men, too, have a mission as peace-builders. In the work of the family as the starting place of peace-making, the father is just as important as the mother. Out in the world, as well, fathers must learn how to listen. Traditionally—though less so today than in the past—women spend more time at home listening to their children. This makes them better listeners than men.

Though mothers today spend less time with children at home, women are still expected to listen as part of their social role. Hearing things that escape masculine attention helps make women effective peacemakers. A good way to build a stronger peace culture in every society is for men to spend more time with children and to learn to listen the way women do.

IKEDA: Yes, you always insist that peace culture begins with listening to others. In this regard, men have a lot to learn from women. Your friend Hazel Henderson insisted in her dialogue with me, *Planetary Citizenship*, that the twenty-first century should be a century of male-female partnership.[3] The thirteenth-century Buddhist reformer Nichiren, the founder of the form of Buddhism practiced by SGI members, taught that "there should be no discrimination . . . , be they men or women."[4] He believed men and women should make equal contributions to society.

Men must respect women. A society that does not value women is doomed to decline and even collapse.

Mutual Influences

THE LOVE OF PARENTS

IKEDA: Through making friends with all kinds of people, I have come to believe that behind every great individual, there is a great mother. Like sunlight, a mother's love can embrace everything. The maternal courage to endure all hardships is a paramount source of strength for children.

I understand that your mother played a big part in your journey toward peace research.

BOULDING: Certainly my mother was a special influence on my life. She wanted everything to be fair, good, and right for everyone. She took concrete steps to assist people around us. For instance, in the summer, she used to invite factory girls on excursions into the mountains for their health.

IKEDA: She set an example for you of caring. Children learn much about life from the daily activities of their mothers. I was born in the Omori district of Tokyo in January 1928. My own mother's cheerfulness, patience, gentleness, and ceaseless industry made a great impression on me. Like many mothers, she constantly admonished me never to lie or cause other people trouble.

BOULDING: My mother was very concerned about old people. When I was small, near our home in Hillside, New Jersey, there was an old people's home. Mother worried about the residents, who just sat there all day long with nothing to do.

To give them some distraction, she would take me to the home and encourage me to sing songs and do little dances for them. She taught me that it is our responsibility to help make people happy. With her love of nature, people, and music, she had an immeasurable influence on me.

IKEDA: She must have been a great mother. Her example reaffirms the mother's important role both in the family and in humanistic education. Because actions speak louder than words, a mother who, busy as she may be, takes the time to work for other people's happiness and makes important contributions to her community becomes the best possible educator for peace and humanity.

What was your father like?

BOULDING: My father had a beautiful singing voice and sometimes performed in local operettas and concerts. On summer lakeside vacations, he and I would swim across the lake together. I was very happy that he liked having me as a swimming partner. So my memory of a loving, caring family—one that related to the community around us, to nature, and to music—is still very strong.

IKEDA: To teach my children the right way to live was my primary parental duty. So I constantly instructed them never to lie and always to keep their promises. About such basics, I was strict. But I avoided scolding them, which I believe stunts a child's growth.

BOULDING: I think many women who are active in society have special relations with their fathers. A good father-daughter relationship is especially important because it encourages women to feel self-confident when they go out into the world. I loved my father very much and was proud of him. And he was proud of me, too.

IKEDA: Father-child relations—especially father-daughter relations—can be particularly strong and deep. This is actually illustrated by a parable in the Lotus Sutra about the dragon king and his daughter, who attained Buddhahood together.[1]

A father and daughter's pride in each other can be a source of great happiness. I get the impression from you of a father and mother eager for your development. Your devotion to peace must have been born from their love and trust.

BOULDING: My mother's teaching that each human being is important helped me to be as self-confident as I am. Discovering the Quakers was another factor. In my student days, I was searching for ways to make the world a more peaceful place. Learning how Quakers worked for peace even in the midst of war was a great discovery. The Quaker community goes by the name of the Religious Society of Friends, and truly I learned the meaning of being a friend in that community.

IKEDA: I, too, prize the wonderful jewel of friendship, which enriches life. Buddhism places high value on friendship as illustrated in this story from the scriptures: Once Shakyamuni Buddha's disciple the venerable Ananda asked him, "Having good friends and practicing among them would be halfway to the mastery of the Buddha Way, would it not?"

Shakyamuni replied: "Having good friends does not constitute the midpoint to the Buddha Way. It constitutes all of the Buddha Way."[2] He saw himself as the good friend to all.

In other words, Buddhism itself can be thought of as the way of friendship—making good friends and becoming a good friend.

BOULDING: Speaking of friendship in those terms, I was inspired by Baroness Maria von Trapp, whose life was the basis for *The Sound of Music*. She, her husband, and their seven children left Austria (in 1938) to escape Nazi persecution. They visited my college while I was a student. While saying little about the danger they had been in, the baroness told us about their peaceful life in the mountains of prewar Austria and her family's intention to contribute to peace by touring the United States making beautiful music.

The von Trapps showed the American people how building peace is possible and reminded us of an important task forgotten in the hectic days of World War II: the work of rebuilding peace ourselves, starting right where we are at the present moment. The whole von Trapp family seemed to have beautiful minds. At a time when I was pondering what to do with my life, their words and music encouraged me to become a peacemaker.

IKEDA: So the von Trapps' pacifist convictions strengthened your sense of mission. Everyone, without exception, has an important mission to fulfill, I believe. People who realize this deep in their lives and fulfill their own unique roles are happy indeed.

One's mission cannot be imposed from without; one must resolutely decide on it oneself. Doing so gives one the courage to accept all challenges and the strength to overcome all hardships.

At the same time, achieving peace is the mission of all humanity—a mission that constantly demands action.

Who else had a big influence on your youth?

BOULDING: Howard and Anna Brinton, directors of Pendle Hill, a Quaker center for contemplation and study, were also inspiring role models. Scholars, teachers, and peace workers, they both were learned, devout, and down-to-earth.

Anna was self-confident and impressive. Both radiant and practical, she knew how to get things done. As a young woman, I learned that there are strong women as well as strong men in the world. Anna taught me self-confidence.

IKEDA: The great Indian poet Rabindranath Tagore wrote, "Women have the vital power more strongly in them than men have."[3] I am also convinced that we must celebrate the strength of women.

The power of women is a mainstay of the SGI. True culture, after all, starts with great respect for women and especially mothers. For the sake of peace, ethnic and religious groups must overcome their cultural differences and come to understand and cooperate with one another; women will undoubtedly play a great role in this.

BOULDING: Women are very active in the Religious Society of Friends as well. To "walk cheerfully over the world, answering that of God in every one,"[4] as George Fox, the founder of the Society of Friends, encouraged us to do, means developing a lot of ingenuity in how to elicit that spirit in all the difficult settings humans face. Women play a key part both in that process and in teaching children to be peacemakers. Since women have had to be good listeners because of their family and community responsibilities, they have also become practical peacemakers. We learn from and teach one another.

IKEDA: Truly hearing what others say is the first step toward mutual understanding and honest dialogue. Even so, disagreements may happen. Sometimes righteous actions are misunderstood and criticized.

But to silently endure injustice is no way to reach solutions. The wisdom and effort to discuss differences of opinion and come to a broad understanding must be persistent until both sides are convinced.

BOULDING: In colonial Pennsylvania, strong mutual respect existed between the American Indians and the Quakers, led by William Penn, for whom the State of Pennsylvania was named. In its early days as a colony, Pennsylvania set an example of how peoples of different cultures can listen to one another, respect one another's needs, and work together for community betterment.

In later times, as more people came over from Europe, the proportion of Quakers in the colony decreased, and conflict increased. Nonetheless, the early practice of listening and dialogue made its own contribution to American culture.

IKEDA: His religious faith enabled Penn to maintain his well-known amicable relations with American Indians.

The Buddhist scriptures include a lovely poetic metaphor to the effect that "when one faces a mirror and makes a bow of obeisance . . . [,] the image in the mirror likewise makes a bow of obeisance to oneself."[5] This metaphor reminds us that a radiant, noble life force is equally inherent in all.

Respecting that radiance in others adds radiance to one's own life. Essential to achieving peace is people of different ideologies understanding and respecting one another.

BOULDING: Exactly so. Quakers are respected because they respect everyone—or try to! When you meet a Quaker, you are respected no matter who you are. No matter who you are and what you do, you will be respected as a child of God. They do not say things like, "Hey, you've got to be like us (if you want to be a pacifist)!"

Peace and Symbiosis

IKEDA: True peace and harmonious symbiosis, indeed, are impossible without mutual respect. I always tell the students of our Soka schools[6] never to build their happiness on the un-happiness of others. The general absence of this teaching is one of the great tragedies of our time.

Theologian Paul Knitter has noted that, while exclusive pursuit of one's own happiness has been considered acceptable in our money-dominated society, traditional religions have consistently taught that one cannot find happiness without contributing to the happiness of others. This message should be spread further throughout the world.

BOULDING: Mired in greed, modern consumer society is far removed from the goals the human spirit truly ought to seek. This is why the peace, environmental-protection, and human-rights movements must redirect our attention to the creation of loving community, to learning, and to dialogue.

I know something of the fine contributions SGI members are making in these areas, where Quakers, too, are doing their part. Dialogue among different religions that share the same goals is vital. By getting to know one another, we can increase our strength to practice our own faiths. Interfaith cooperation must be a key aspect of social and spiritual movements.

IKEDA: Person-to-person dialogue with a sense of humility must be made basic to all intercultural and interreligious exchange. In June 1991, shortly after the reunification of Germany, I met with Richard von Weizsäcker, philosopher and then president of the Federal Republic of Germany, who was at that time struggling to demolish the invisible wall that still separated the peoples of East and West Germany. He impressed on me that mutual respect and direct contact, free of all condescension, were indispensable to this monumental undertaking.

Conducted steadily, repeatedly, and tenaciously, one-on-one dialogue based on respect can advance the development of a global society of peace and harmonious coexistence.

Norway's Cooperative Spirit

Uses of Adversity

IKEDA: Some say that we are, to a large extent, what our environment makes us. Norway, the land of your birth, must have had a profound influence on you.

Tsunesaburo Makiguchi, the first Soka Gakkai president and founder of Soka education,[1] stressed the importance of how we relate to our local environment. Similarly, Buddhism teaches the *oneness* of life and its environment. From this perspective, the nation creates the individual, and the individual creates the nation. I imagine that both the land of Norway and the spirit of its people affected your character deeply.

BOULDING: I was born in Oslo in 1920. But since I left the country when I was only three years old, what I remember of my early childhood is mostly what my mother told me about the way of life there and how the Norwegians valued equality, how creative they were on social issues, and how they managed to live on their mountainous peninsula. Lack of arable land means that sea products constitute a large portion of the Norwegian diet. My Norwegian identity was very real for me as a child.

IKEDA: I formed unforgettable impressions of Norway and its people when I visited Oslo in October 1964. The Vigeland Sculpture Park, famous for its sculpture by Gustav Vigeland, remains particularly vivid in my mind's eye.

The Norwegians, I felt, are tough in mind and body, individualistic, and creative. They have set a great example for the world of how seemingly adverse circumstances provide us the precious chance to manifest real value.

Buddhism, too, stresses never being defeated by our hardships, working for the happiness of others, and succeeding in our lives and society. Buddhist practitioners who courageously live this way will experience Buddhahood as a reality in their lives. Wherever we wage our struggle becomes our place of victory, our realm of eternal happiness.

BOULDING: All the things Mother told me about Norway related to how well people were taken care of there. Norway has always had a very strong welfare society. It has cared for its people and has been friendly with other countries.

IKEDA: I admire the good care Norway takes of its citizens. Everything—including politics and economics—should be founded on serving the people. This is the goal we should struggle to attain for all people.

Norway has a history of diplomacy and multinational cooperation. Trygve Lie, the first elected secretary-general of the United Nations, was Norwegian. He worked energetically to promote UN participation in peacekeeping operations and to assist developing nations. Norwegian minister of foreign affairs

Johan Jorgen Holst mediated the discussions that led to the Oslo Accords[2] of September 1993, which gave us hope on the rocky road to Israeli-Palestinian peace. In an interview following the signing of the accords, Holst emphasized the role of a neutral third-party nation to bridge gaps. This idea was certainly in keeping with Norwegian tradition.

BOULDING: As a child, I made up my mind that if there should ever be another war, I would go to Norway and be safe because the Norwegians would not be fighting. But the Nazis invaded Norway during World War II. That happened when I was in college, and I was shocked to realize that my safe place was gone.

The Norwegians did not confront armed force with violence. Instead, they created an underground communications network throughout Norway involving non-cooperation with the occupiers and taking care of one another. All Nazi orders were responded to with a polite but stubborn refusal to submit. This is the strategy they developed.

"ATTACHMENT TO DIFFERENCE"

IKEDA: The history of the Norwegians' nonviolent resistance to the Nazis reveals their true spirit. While the rugged terrain led the people of each valley to develop a strong, unique identity, it ultimately bred a spirit of unity. The Norwegians' geographic and cultural diversity made their grassroots resistance all the more effective.

BOULDING: The communications networks of the Norwegian nonviolent resistance made it possible to educate children just as in peacetime. The resistance proved splendidly effective. The plans the Nazis thought would work in Norway miscarried.

IKEDA: It was a victory for a grassroots network of ordinary people. Even the most overwhelming authority could not crush the inner fortress of peace the Norwegians had built. This strong fortress of the spirit would not fall. What a great historical example of the people's triumph over authoritarian forces!

Nichiren struggled against the tyrannical authorities of thirteenth-century Japan for the happiness of the people. He addressed these words to the supreme authority of the time: "Even if it seems that, because I was born in the ruler's domain, I follow him in my actions, I will never follow him in my heart."[3]

UNESCO included this passage in a selection of words of wisdom prepared under the direction of Jeanne Hersch in the book *Birthright of Man*. It was published in 1969 to commemorate the twentieth anniversary of the Universal Declaration of Human Rights (1948). Nichiren's quote is found under the heading "Limits to authority" in the section "Conditional submission, supremacy of conscience" in the chapter "Limitations on power." A great soul is so strong that it will not bow before any authority.

What other factors enabled the Norwegians to resist the Nazis so successfully?

BOULDING: Over the centuries, the Norwegians built up strong regional communities with rules for coping with differences. Although we did not use the words at the time, looking back now, I see that what they were doing was building a peace culture across all the intermountain valleys.

IKEDA: They indeed created an open network of dialogue within and among their local communities. In the world today, unfortunately, shallow attachment to national, racial, and religious differences is our fundamental illness that needs to be cured. In my 1993 speech at Harvard University, titled

"Mahayana Buddhism and Twenty-first-Century Civilization," I argued that conquering "attachment to difference" is both the *sine qua non* of candid dialogue and the first step toward lasting peace and universal human rights.[4] Attaining this goal entails creating the kind of peace culture toward which your peace work has long aimed.

The Light of Hope and Courage

BOULDING: By the time I was in college, I realized that, if there is going to be a peaceful world, we have to make it ourselves. Wherever they are, people must know how to make peace. I first came to peace research as a homemaker, mother of five, and community volunteer, then as a scholar-activist-networker.

IKEDA: As I mentioned earlier (see Conversation One), the central feature of the SGI's movement is the discussion meeting, in which members of local communities gather to talk about Buddhist philosophy. We are thus confident that ours is a truly grassroots movement for peace and human rights.

After the oppression inflicted on us by the wartime militarists, the Soka Gakkai rose like a phoenix from the ashes under Toda's leadership. Through the Buddhist philosophy of peace and happiness, we brought the light of hope and courage to a postwar society afflicted with unspeakable suffering, poverty, and sickness.

People who know in their bones the misery and folly of war appreciate the blessing of peace all the more. When they grow strong and wise enough to lead society, such people can lay the foundation for true democracy. This is the basis on which we can end the cruelty of war. The SGI is united for peace and the well-being of *all* humanity.

BOULDING: Today, as people lose hope and war rages in many parts of the world, it might seem that we will never know peace again. Actually, however, nineteen or twenty nations have renounced maintaining armed forces. We should know and honor these zones of peace. This should encourage us to prize our transnational peace and nonviolence networks and to work actively with our sisters and brothers around the world to make the whole earth a peace zone.

IKEDA: In 1948, Costa Rica eliminated its armed forces. This was owing to the wisdom of its farsighted president José Figueres Ferrer. His son, José María Figueres Olsen, became president in 1994. He is a dear friend of mine.

I spoke at the opening ceremony for the SGI exhibition "Nuclear Arms: Threat to Humanity" in San José, Costa Rica, in June 1996. With the happy voices of children coming from the adjacent Children's Museum, I began: "The sight and sound of these youngsters, boisterous and full of vitality, is the very image of peace. It is here that we can find the power to stem the tide of nuclear arms. It is here we can find hope."

Children are emissaries from the future. The outlook is bright for a society full of smiling, hopeful children. It is our responsibility as adults to cherish their untrammeled vitality and develop their limitless potential to the utmost. This is the starting point for everything.

Early Roots of Peace

INTO THE ESSENCE OF THINGS

BOULDING: Thank you so much for the book of your photographs you recently gave me. In the one of tulips, the viewer steps into the world of the picture—in this case, into "tulipness." In a sense, you become a tulip; you feel the world as a tulip. To me, that is what art and poetry are all about: to enter into the essence of things.

Another photograph, of the moon, is a window on the universe. It suggests how everything exists within us: the stars, the moonlight, the brilliance of the sun, and all their wisdom. Your picture of the moon really says it all.

IKEDA: In my spare moments at home or on the road, I enjoy taking photographs, mostly of nature or urban scenes. I feel it is a conversation. Buddhism teaches that our inner lives and the great life of the universe are ultimately united. Tulips, moon, sun—all are unique. At the same time, all life arises from the great universal force of life. The camera can capture the mystic rhythm and natural drama of light and color instant by instant.

BOULDING: You capture the spirituality of the city. For example, one photograph shows a grove of trees in downtown Tokyo. The two belong together. In other words, there would be no city if there were no trees. Today, cities overlook the connection. They consider themselves self-sufficient and have no need of trees. But actually, in a sense, buildings are only dead materials, which can be brought to life—as in this picture—by the addition of cherry trees in bloom. Your photographs help me remember the year we lived in Japan and that very special season of the cherry blossoms.

IKEDA: Your generous praise aside, I sense your power of observation, love of nature, and photographic eye, which I deeply respect.

Can we return to your youth? As the mother of peace research and a parent yourself, you have set an encouraging example for young women and mothers. I understand that you decided to become a peace scholar during your time in college. What did you dream of becoming as a child?

BOULDING: I did not have any burning ambitions as a child. I simply enjoyed living. I loved to play at being a teacher from a very young age, so it is not surprising that I ended up as a teacher. In my early years, I never imagined being a researcher. What did you dream of becoming?

IKEDA: In my youth in totally militarized Japan, children were not free to dream. I was three when the so-called Manchuria

Incident[1] occurred. World War II started when I was thirteen and did not end until I was seventeen.

We were taught that selfless devotion, to sacrifice one's life for the nation, constituted the highest morality. At one time, I even thought of volunteering for the air force. But I really wanted to become a journalist or novelist. That is why, after the war, I was delighted to find work as an editor for a youth magazine published by my mentor.

Where were you on December 7, 1941, when the Pacific War broke out?

BOULDING: Kenneth and I were gathered for a community performance of Handel's *Messiah* in Princeton, New Jersey, that afternoon. That shocking announcement made it a very moving occasion. Later, we were greatly disturbed to hear that the United States was at war.

IKEDA: Our family heard the radio announcement of the war's start together. I still remember my father sighing, "So, at last, war with America has begun."

BOULDING: I was so glad that Kenneth and I were already married, because he already had done a great deal of work toward disarmament. Since I was ten years younger than he, I considered myself lucky to be his partner and to be able to learn from him.

THE BEST TEACHERS

IKEDA: Who among your teachers was especially memorable?

BOULDING: I have strong memories of several teachers at Douglass College who stimulated me and gave me a lot to think about. I also recall one high school teacher who instilled a deep love of poetry in me. He shared his passions and wanted us to have our own poetic experiences and to write our own interpretations of poetry.

Teachers who are really interested in what students are thinking make a difference in life. The teachers I remember best were genuinely concerned about what I thought. This influenced my approach to students when I became a teacher later.

IKEDA: As an old Chinese saying has it, "Teachers of book learning are easy to find; people who teach how to be a human being are hard to come by." In my experience, what remains longest in the memory is not the knowledge conveyed but the teacher's warmth, encouragement, and humanity.

BOULDING: I agree. Nature is a teacher, too. We had an apple tree in our backyard at one of the houses we lived in during our years in Hillside, New Jersey. It was my special place. When I wanted some time to myself, I would climb the tree, taking a book and maybe lunch up with me, and read and daydream for hours. That tree still has a special place in my heart.

IKEDA: I, too, have an unforgettable tree. When I was small, we lived near Tokyo Bay. In the autumn, I loved to climb a pomegranate tree in our yard to see the thick skin of the fruit break open, revealing juicy seeds inside.

Before I entered elementary school, I was briefly bedridden with pneumonia. When I was on the mend, my mother told me: "Look at that pomegranate tree. It's supposed to hate the sea breeze and sandy soil around here, but still it blooms and bears fruit year upon year. You may be weak now, but you're sure to grow as strong as that tree someday."

BOULDING: When I compare humans and trees, it seems to me that trees stand on their heads, so to speak. Their roots, which absorb information and food, go deep into the ground, while their branches point up to the sky. It could be said that trees talk to one another root to root, while their legs dance in the air! Even now, on my early morning walks, I sometimes see the trees that way.

IKEDA: A powerful poetic image indeed. Poets delve into and express the great life force permeating the human being, society, and the universe. Poetry becomes the wings of limitless creativity for the human soul and manifests the spirit and wisdom enabling us to live to our highest potential. The loss of the poetic spirit is one reason for the desolation of our modern society.

Returning to your research, how did having children influence your work?

BOULDING: I saw raising children as peace work.

IKEDA: Indeed it is. You mentioned that you had your first child five years after your marriage. It must have been hard to find time for your research while raising a baby.

BOULDING: A group of mothers in the Quaker community where we lived worked out a system for giving one another free days. We took turns caring for all the little ones in our own homes. For instance, I would have all the children on a certain day; and all the other mothers would have free time for their own activities.

IKEDA: In the Soka Gakkai, we have a young mothers' group that does the same kind of thing. The mothers arrange their schedules to enable one another to attend appointments or Buddhist study meetings without their children in tow. Other women, too, offer the mothers assistance.

BOULDING: I arranged my schedule to participate in my husband's seminars. On seminar days, I would carry a coffeepot from home to the Center for Research on Conflict Resolution (at the University of Michigan) and make and serve coffee during the proceedings. I took notes during the seminars and later wrote them up. They became valuable sources of information about the early days of developing the field of conflict resolution.

IKEDA: Your life has been the model of what we in the SGI call value-creation (*soka*) and how to use time creatively.

Lifelong Learning and Growth

BOULDING: People sent lots of letters to Kenneth and his colleagues inquiring about this new Center for Research on Conflict Resolution. Neither Kenneth nor his colleagues had time to respond. So I created a newsletter made up of the contents of all those letters, typing it up myself. I titled it *The Peace Research Newsletter* and sent it out to everyone who wrote in. The International Peace Research Association eventually grew out of that newsletter.

IKEDA: For one mother to have helped create a worldwide peace network is an enduring achievement of ingenuity and effort.

BOULDING: Feeling that sociology was the field that would help me understand conflict resolution, I took a course with Reuben Hill, the chairman of the Sociology Department at the University of Iowa. At first, as the babies started coming and we moved to the University of Michigan, I continued taking courses, completing a master's degree. But with the fourth child, it became too difficult. Naming the fourth Philip Daniel, I told everyone he was my PhD.

IKEDA: You got your doctorate after your children had grown up a bit.

BOULDING: Yes. But I documented the peace movement that was growing up around us and studied how children responded to it. I used a corner of our bedroom as my research office. Once the five children were in school, I realized I could be more effective with more training, so I went back to school and took a doctorate. Live-in students helped with childcare when I began doing more international travel. And, of course, the Quaker community was also a part of our family life.

IKEDA: Reading has always been an important part of learning—and living—for you. What kind of books did you like when you were young?

BOULDING: My early years, I mostly read biographies. I was an immigrant child, and our teachers talked a lot about immigrant children and how they could make good lives in the United States. Now I spend a lot of time reading books on governance, and I read mystery stories for relaxation. Of course, I love reading my husband's poetry. I read some of his sonnets—especially the ones he wrote in the last two years of his life—every day. His presence is very real to me.

I read history a lot, too. Even today, in my eighties, I do not know nearly as much about world history as I should. I have always enjoyed reading Arnold Toynbee's books.

IKEDA: His name brings back many fond memories for me. The ten days we spent in dialogue together (in the early 1970s) began my series of dialogues with many leading thinkers of the world.

BOULDING: Toynbee thought that humanity would move into a more spiritual state of being. I think he was overly optimistic but can understand his taking such a view. A lot of other people, too, believe we are undergoing a spiritual revolution. Well, we *are*, but we are still in the childhood of the human race. We must never forget that the spiritual potential is there.

A World Without Armies

IKEDA: Although the level of our technological achievements has risen sharply, the gap between our technological abilities and ethical standards has never been as wide as now. Toynbee and I agreed that we must persevere toward a world in which respect for life is the supreme value.

What advice can you offer young people on where to begin their journey to the future?

BOULDING: First, they must be able to conceive of a world without armies. Then they must start figuring out ways to make such a world happen. Although many people find the idea unimaginable, we must first have a mental picture of a highly diverse world functioning without military establishments and dealing creatively with conflict. My husband said over and over again, "What exists is possible." Think of all the places in the world where people do live in peace! A really good, working system is both possible and achievable.

IKEDA: A splendid message for youth. People tend to be deluded into thinking that the present is unchangeable and the future is already set in stone. They proceed under the false impression that current realities will never change. But, keeping our eyes on present realities, we must envision a peaceful future.

Mahatma Gandhi, Martin Luther King Jr., and my friend Mikhail Gorbachev have proven that nonviolence, often considered a mere ideal, is indeed a practical way to realize peace. Both a witness to the power games of the Cold War and a firm believer in the possibilities of a new age, Gorbachev accomplished what many considered impossible in helping bring the Cold War to an end. He showed that the strong popular desire for peace propels inevitable change. So with confidence that people who can imagine the future will be the ones to create the future, let's continue our efforts to realize a world overflowing with the happy smiles of mothers and children.

The Core of a Peace Culture

SECRETS OF GOOD HEALTH

IKEDA: Your work for peace has kept you busy for many years, yet you remain youthful and active. What is the secret to your good health?

BOULDING: Well, I take a walk every morning before breakfast. I love to meditate as I walk among the trees down a hill near our building. I greet every growing thing and give time to quiet reflection. Every day, I take a nap after lunch. Getting more rest is essential at my time of life.

IKEDA: My wife constantly urges me to walk in the morning.

In Shakyamuni's time, by the way, walking was widely considered to be a prime practice for maintaining one's health. Buddhist scriptures describe the virtues of walking, benefits that are now recognized by modern medicine: It strengthens your resistance to sickness and improves your digestion and reasoning abilities. As is well known, Immanuel Kant prized walking and reflection, going out at set times every day.

BOULDING: I also dress simply and eat plain food.

IKEDA: I suspect that your passion for peace, too, contributes to your good health. Isn't the supreme rule for good health to abandon selfishness and devote ourselves to something worthwhile? In Nichiren Buddhism, for instance, devotion to the Mystic Law[1] is said to deepen our youthfulness. Undeniably, people who continue to pursue noble goals and live altruistically can stay young at heart as the years go by. You illustrate Hermann Hesse's principle that maturity rejuvenates. I hope you will stay forever healthy and continue to speak vigorously for the sake of a glorious peace culture and century of women.

Cultivating Harmony

IKEDA: The United Nations is a linchpin of world peace. How were your years with UNESCO and the United Nations University?

BOULDING: I worked a little with the United Nations in the disarmament divisions, but mostly I worked with UNESCO. Then, in 1980, I was appointed to the UNU Council, which has its main center in Tokyo. I served on the council for five years. The United Nations University helps link the international academic community with the ongoing activities of the United Nations itself. This is very important work. It is my hope that these connections will continue to grow.

IKEDA: At the time of your wedding, your husband worked for the Department of Economic and Social Affairs of the League of Nations at Princeton, so you also had a connection with the League.

BOULDING: I would go to seminars and open meetings so I could learn more about what was going on.

IKEDA: Inazo Nitobe, under-secretary-general of the League of Nations, was a friend of Makiguchi's and agreed with his doctrine of Soka education. Nitobe founded the International Committee on Intellectual Cooperation, the forerunner of UNESCO.

BOULDING: I am pleased to learn of this connection between two who played important roles in the League of Nations and the Soka Gakkai respectively.

Experiences as a young mother with community groups concerned about World War II helped me discover that local organizations, such as churches and civic groups, often were connected to national offices and even to international head-quarters. These could take their concerns for peace and justice directly to the United Nations. That discovery of international NGOs[2] really shaped my development as a peace activist.

IKEDA: People tend to think of the United Nations as some-how remote. Actually, it is an organization for the people. The preamble of its charter begins, "We the peoples of the United Nations. . . ."

For the people of Japan, UNESCO and UNICEF (the United Nations Children's Fund) are the most familiar institutions of the UN network. UNESCO, where you played an important role, is well known for its World Heritage mission, and its former director-general was a Japanese, Koichiro Matsuura. Japan joined UNESCO in 1951 before becoming a member of the United Nations and before the conclusion of the Treaty of Peace with Japan. The UNESCO Clubs, which support UNESCO work, were born in Sendai, Japan.

BOULDING: UNESCO plays an important role by promoting reciprocal learning and understanding of the great diversity of cultures among UN member states.

IKEDA: The cultivation of harmony, symbiosis, and mutual acceptance forms the core of peace culture. As you have said, however, "The creative management of differences is at the core of peace culture; in other words, it is not a culture without conflict" (see Appendix One).[3]

How did you become involved with UNESCO, which upholds and advances the ideal of peace culture?

BOULDING: As secretary general of the International Peace Research Association (in the late 1980s), I worked very closely with UNESCO, which helped us develop international networks among different countries then just beginning to grasp the concept of peace research. It put out a marvelous series of publications on issues of world peace and problem solving. I used those books in my peace study classes in the United States. I am afraid, however, that they are not used as much as they should be.

The UNESCO Charter and Peace Culture

IKEDA: You maintained your connection with UNESCO?

BOULDING: I worked with UNESCO on the concept of developing peace culture as the idea began to grow. It was very important work, and a number of fine projects have come out of the peace-culture program.

IKEDA: The history of UNESCO can be seen as the history of building peace cultures. The opening passage of the preamble to its constitution states, "Since wars begin in the minds of men, it is in the minds of men that the defenses of peace must be constructed." This resonates profoundly with our belief in the SGI that the "human revolution" of one individual can reform society and the whole world. When I met Federico Mayor Zaragoza, UNESCO director-general, he was pleased that the ideals of UNESCO and the SGI agree.

BOULDING: As you know, the UN General Assembly declared the years from 2001–10 the International Decade for a Culture of Peace and Non-violence for the Children of the World. I was very happy to be a part of that whole process and have continued to stay involved in the development of those programs.

EMPOWERING THE UNITED NATIONS

IKEDA: As an NGO registered with UNESCO, the SGI has worked hard to publicize the International Decade for a Culture of Peace and Non-violence. This effort has included our "Women and the Culture of Peace" exhibition (see Conversation One), as well as our "World Boys and Girls Art Exhibition" and "Read Me a Story!" exhibition, which showcased children's storybooks and folk tales from around the world. Our exhibition "Building a Culture of Peace for the Children of the World" was meanwhile a great success at the UN Headquarters (February 2004). At its opening, UN Under-Secretary-General Anwarul Karim Chowdhury said he was very happy that young people could visit the exhibition to learn the significance of peace culture.

BOULDING: Your support is encouraging. The peace-culture program must go on. But unfortunately, it is still confined within the circle of peace activists. Popular ignorance of the United Nations' work is one of the things that weaken it. I want people to know more about it. UNESCO has published wonderful material. If it were widely used, things would change a lot.

IKEDA: The SGI continues to do its best to support the United Nations. We feel that ordinary people must support the United Nations at the grassroots level for it to be truly effective. When I met former UN secretary-general Boutros Boutros-Ghali, he strongly agreed on this point.

We have always believed in the central importance of the United Nations. Some criticize the organization as impotent or even as a sham. Admittedly, it has many problems. But we have no other internationally cooperative organization to replace it.

I am deeply convinced that working with and further empowering the UN system is a practical approach to peace. What do you consider most important in reinvigorating the United Nations?

BOULDING: There are several things. We need many more well-trained peacemakers, especially women. As you know, the United Nations has resolved that women must participate and be fully involved in all efforts for the maintenance and promotion of peace. In the years to come, women will be increasingly called on to carry out those duties.

IKEDA: You are referring to Security Council Resolution 1325 (2000), which is epoch-making as the first legal document from the UN Security Council to call upon all parties engaged in armed conflict to fully respect the rights of women and girls. It also acknowledges the role of women in preventing conflict and achieving peace.

Reform is needed in many other areas as well, including the composition of the Security Council, civic participation, and financial affairs. Anand Panyarachun, former prime minister of Thailand and head of the UN High-level Panel on Threats, Challenges and Change, once told me that, although we cannot expect the United Nations to solve everything, the world has been improved by the United Nations. His panel presented its proposals to the United Nations in 2004, and I, too, have proposed reforms on many occasions, including in my annual peace proposals. Indeed, there are already plenty of proposals.

What we need now is political will and action. Then, with the pooling of grassroots enthusiasm, we can help the United Nations move forward. The year 2005 marked the sixtieth anniversary of its formation; the time has come for clear deadlines on its reformation.

BOULDING: I hope that Japan will play a more prominent role in the United Nations. As the United Nations University is located in Japan, it is already playing a part. But I think it would be wonderful for Japan to devote more time to UN diplomacy. Plenty of work remains to be done—especially in relation to America, which seems in recent years to have turned its back on its earlier path of peace diplomacy.

IKEDA: International society must move in the direction of multinational cooperation and the rule of law. Toward this, the United Nations has plenty to do. Its importance is only going to increase. Sadako Ogata, former UN high commissioner for refugees, has called on Japan, in particular, to become a great humanitarian nation. We of the SGI have been insisting on the same thing for years.

Makiguchi believed that the coming age must not be locked into the pursuit of military, economic, and political supremacy. Instead, it must be one of "humanitarian competition," focusing on human symbiosis and harmony in various fields, including culture, education, human rights, and ethics. Admired for its Peace Constitution[4] throughout the world, Japan must now assume more leadership in the creation of peace culture.

Beyond the Win-Lose Mentality

GREEN SIDE, BLACK SIDE

IKEDA: For your eighty-fourth birthday in 2004, you wrote a poem that moved me deeply:

> Now I'm eighty-four,
> And there's more:
> Before me is a door.
> When it opens wide,
> I'll see the other side.
> There lies All Creation—
> What a cause for celebration!

BOULDING: Thank you for quoting my poem. In spite of all the dark tidings of recent days, we know better days will come. I hope our conversations inspire hope for a brighter future and are part of the larger theme of peace education for young people, who will help create the future.

IKEDA: This reminds me of your book *The Future: Images and Processes*, which you sent me.

BOULDING: Kenneth and I made that a joint project.

IKEDA: The book includes interviews conducted in 1979 with American teenagers. You asked them what they thought the world would be like in 2005.
One answered:

> This is the year 2005. The Earth is green and fertile on one side and black, smoky, and polluted on the other. Nothing can grow on that side of the world. On the green side, kids are playing all day and all night. We never sleep. On the black side, there are just robots wishing that they could play.[1]

BOULDING: The contrast between the green and black sides of the earth expresses in extreme terms the North-South problem facing the world at present.
As the economic gap widens between the industrial nations, which I call the One-Third World, and the developing nations, the Two-Thirds World, living conditions in the Two-Thirds World grow steadily worse. Chronic malnutrition is widespread.

GLOBAL APARTHEID?

IKEDA: The rich-poor gap is one of the most profound problems in the world today. The teenager's answer to your question continues:

There is a wall separating the black side from the green side of the Earth. The wall is called the wall of justice. It keeps the pollution on the black side. Scientists say that in 10 years we will have to build a new wall of justice or move to the moon.[2]

In addressing the World Summit on Sustainable Development (August 2002), South Africa President Thabo Mvuyelwa Mbeki, whom I have met twice, warned that the rich-poor, North-South gap amounts to global apartheid. Where should we look for solutions to this grave and complex problem?

BOULDING: The problem is indeed complex but looks simpler from a different viewpoint. We know far too little about the South, but the people who live there have wonderful varieties of lifeways. The indigenous people of the world have highly developed knowledge of their environments.

IKEDA: The people of industrialized nations know far too little of the peoples of developing nations. We have failed to learn from their venerable and wonderful traditions, cultures, and life-wisdom.

BOULDING: In my writings, I refer to the "ten thousand societies"[3] that are spread across the 191 nations of the UN system. The richness of their cultures needs to be known by peoples of the industrialized states.

IKEDA: The Indian agronomist Monkombu Sambasivan Swaminathan has told me that modern science still must learn traditional wisdom and ecological concern. Traditional wisdom is humankind's great treasure, a rich spiritual source. Swaminathan has worked hard to empower farmers and women, those whose social position in India remains low. He has made various useful proposals and, side by side with the ordinary people, striven to empower those who suffer most, beginning with the very poor. I would love to see similar efforts in many other parts of the world.

BOULDING: Things are beginning to change. There are people in the industrialized nations who are trying to learn from indigenous people's traditional methods of cultivating the land and their rich cultural diversity.

In the past, certain pharmaceutical companies have shamelessly and without concern preyed on indigenous people's knowledge of medicinal plants. They had no right to do that. This is a time for dialogue and mutual learning, and a number of NGOs focused on peace, social justice, and environmental issues are leading the way in this. Many women's groups, I am happy to say, are leading the way.

INTERDEPENDENCE AND WELFARE

IKEDA: As you say, mutual learning in the spirit of humility among peoples of diverse cultures, traditions, and religions is what the world today most needs. The industrialized capitalist nations tend to take it as gospel that if some people win, others must inevitably lose. The fact is that as long as there are losers, there can be no true winners. We must change our way of categorizing people into "winners" and "losers" based on the assumption that there must always be losers.

BOULDING: Win-lose language has indeed led human beings astray. We must learn to recognize that we are *interdependent*, not only with all humans but also with all of nature, all living things.

IKEDA: The Buddhist doctrine of dependent origination teaches that all things are interconnected, all things influence one another. Based on this interconnectedness, it behooves us to create a win-win world.

All people are worthy of respect, no matter where or how they live. The mission of education and religion is to develop in people empathy for other citizens of the world who are different from themselves.

Without doubt, the North-South gap even plays out within the industrialized nations themselves. To make sure there are no losers in either the world at large or at the local level, we must take the side of the underprivileged and develop better social systems.

In Japan, where society is steadily "graying," social security, pensions, and the health-care system are topics of extensive public debate. In the future, how do you think welfare systems would best work?

BOULDING: Indigenous peoples all have welfare-sharing systems and much wisdom about sharing. I think that, by and large, the so-called developed people of the One-Third World of the West, as mass production and the corresponding consumer society have taken shape, have destroyed a lot of that sharing by exploiting and creating inequalities.

Some states have liberal welfare systems. For instance, everyone in Norway, including housewives, is entitled to two weeks vacation per year. At least, that has been true in the past; I am not sure whether it still is today.

IKEDA: The welfare systems of Northern Europe are esteemed worldwide.

BOULDING: Yes, they are. But high levels of public welfare can also involve abuses.

IKEDA: Too much welfare can dull people's motivation and enervate society. We must determine how, based on the conditions in each country, to create a society enabling everyone to live fully and happily in keeping with the best of human nature.

On the Meaning of Life

BOULDING: Some countries do better than others. It is easy to admire or criticize the welfare systems of countries other than your own. The real question is, however, whether a country's welfare system is better than it used to be, whether lifeways have improved, and whether the people themselves take responsibility as citizens.

IKEDA: That is an important perspective. In Japan, during the rapid economic growth following World War II, the government downplayed welfare. But despite dramatic advances in the economy as a whole, grinding poverty was by no means eradicated.

BOULDING: Riches, materialism, and consumerism are totally false values that run counter to real human happiness. People who only want to get richer and richer should know better. They think if they get richer, they will feel happier, but they may find there is little of real substance or value in their lives.

IKEDA: Contemporary society fails to question the purpose of life and what real purpose wealth should serve. I agree that happiness cannot be measured in terms of money, having known many economically blessed but unhappy people. It is the role of education, philosophy, and religion to teach this fundamental lesson.

Toynbee said:

I hold that the goal of education ought to be religious, not
mercenary. Education ought to be a search for an understanding of the meaning and the purpose of life and for discovering the right way to live. The right spiritual way is, I believe,
fundamentally identical for all human beings.[4]

In examining the meaning of life, we must turn our eyes to
the religious aspect of human life. Indeed, isn't this where we
find religion's main mission? Religion should not be escapism. It
should help us challenge and overcome life's hardships. Religion
exists to cultivate in the human heart strength and a deeper
understanding of the meaning of life.

Breaking the Chain of Violence

THE FALLACY OF A "JUST WAR"

IKEDA: I understand you are reading Gandhi's complete works. That is quite a challenge.

BOULDING: It is. His greatness impresses me deeply.

IKEDA: Your continuing eagerness to learn and develop shows how young you are at heart. In the name of peace, I hope to remain youthful, too. I want to go on learning, engaging in dialogue, and striving to eliminate misery from the world.

Though they seem to mention peace a lot, politicians, scholars, and the mass media tend, in fact, to be far removed from real issues of peace. In our violent world, it is the ordinary people who always suffer the most. Our task is to reduce the escalation of violence we have seen in our world since the September 11, 2001, terrorist attacks in the United States.

BOULDING: With those attacks, the American people experienced in their own country for the first time war and violence of the kinds other peoples have known for years. As you know, America was in large part responsible for the devastation and miseries suffered by the people of Hiroshima and Nagasaki, as well as in parts of Europe and elsewhere.

IKEDA: I experienced the bombing of Japan during World War II and lost my oldest brother in the war. The indescribable horror of war is thus deeply etched on my mind.

Let me take this opportunity to express my deepest regrets for the lives lost in the September 11 attacks. But I feel the same way about all lives lost to war and violence—including those lives lost in Afghanistan and Iraq.

BOULDING: I do, too. I really felt sick at heart that Americans did not realize what sheltered lives they had led and that September 11 should seem an unprecedented disaster to them, when it reflects the human loss in many parts of the world.

IKEDA: Empathy with others' pain must form the core of our approach. As long as human beings resort to violence to solve problems, they will forever be trapped in this cycle of hatred and violence. Some people argue that sacrificing others and taking lives are permissible as means to a greater end. We must disabuse everyone of this notion.

Because it undervalues life, the culture of war should be fundamentally questioned. My friend Joseph Rotblat would repeat the adage, "If you want peace, prepare for peace" (*Si vis pacem para pacem*). It is wrong to assume that peace can ever be realized through the means of war.

BOULDING: In my opinion, there can be no "just war," because war generates war. It solves no problems. None at all! Nor can it create the conditions for peace. The *last* thing it does is create the conditions for peace.

The January 1945 fire bombing of Dresden was horrible. Then, when Hiroshima and Nagasaki suffered atomic attacks, I thought to myself, "Humans are really capable of anything now!" Ever since the bombing of Dresden, I have sensed what I call a process of moral numbing in regard to acts of war.

IKEDA: Many people still argue that, though tragic, actions that may take tens or hundreds of thousands of lives may be unavoidable. Some even claim they can be useful because they can shorten conflicts. Such attitudes are perilous.

FEELING OTHERS' FEELINGS

BOULDING: Historically speaking, World War II was the first time that huge numbers of civilians were bombed. In attacks of this kind, opponents obviously never come face to face.

IKEDA: Recent dramatic developments in weapons technology exacerbate this. People are becoming divorced from the horrible reality of wartime killing, as when we see on television missile launchings but not their tragic impact. To counter this, we must be able to imagine others' suffering. We must cultivate the empathy to share and even alleviate their pain.

Of course, we must rigorously expose and protest those cowardly terrorist attacks that are occurring time and again throughout the world. But we must also try to see the fundamental causes behind them.

BOULDING: A feeling of desperation leads to terrorism. Terrorists think that no one listens to them and that their only recourse is violence. If they saw another way, they might take it. But they see none.

IKEDA: Poverty and a sense of its injustice have too often engendered terrorism. What would you consider the best way to eliminate such tragedy from the world?

BOULDING: Listening and bringing people together in dialogue and getting to know what kind of world they live in.

IKEDA: Dealing with poverty and injustice is a long-term endeavor. But we can start listening right now. Dialogue is the best way forward.

BOULDING: What are the terrorists thinking about? What is on their minds? Have we ever asked them? No! We just put them in jail.

IKEDA: Instead of imposing our own version of wisdom, the spirit of dialogue requires us to put ourselves in others' shoes. We cannot overstate the fact that this spirit is the foundation of peace culture.

My friend Wole Soyinka, the first African Nobel laureate for literature, once reminded me that the simplest, clearest justice is to do to others only what you would have them do to you. He added that imagining things from the other party's viewpoint is essential to justice.

BOULDING: Peace culture begins with learning from the wisdom of other peoples. In the past, colonists would have done well to learn from the natives of the regions they invaded. For example, forest dwellers could have instructed them in ways of dealing with strangers. It is often a custom among forest dwellers to send a member of their group out to meet a stranger. After an exchange of greetings, the local person asks the stranger who he is and why he has come. Then the stranger is invited to sit in a circle with the locals so that they can come to know one another. This ceremonious greeting and interviewing take the place of, say, shooting strangers on sight. This way, both sides can reveal what is on their minds.

VIOLENCE IS NOT HARDWIRED

IKEDA: Speaking of the wisdom of indigenous people reminds me of the Iroquois (also known as the Haudenosaunee). Women had considerable power in Iroquois tradition, choosing the chiefs of their clans and removing said chiefs when necessary.

According to many anthropologists, women were afforded roles of central importance in prehistoric culture. This was believed to be out of respect for their bringing forth and nurturing life. War was minimized in cooperative societies in which the sexes were considered equal. When many societies became male-dominated, warfare increased dramatically. This situation has persisted until today.

This history—plus the existence of totally peaceful cultures of indigenous peoples—suggests that the accepted idea that violence is instinctive, therefore ineradicable, is incorrect. In fact, the Seville Statement on Violence, issued by twenty scientists in 1986, denounces as scientifically wrong the concept that war is hardwired into human nature.

BOULDING: The idea that violence is instinctive is nonsense. As we have said, the UN General Assembly declared the years from 2001–10 the International Decade for a Culture of Peace and Non-violence for the Children of the World (see Conversation Five). Sadly, it has not been widely observed. Still, in many countries, we are learning about already existing peace cultures. Over the centuries, people in all societies have worked out ways of dealing with injustice, conflict, and difference.

History books include little about peace processes; they concentrate on the excitement aroused by the development of increasingly destructive weapons. The important thing is for people to learn about and recreate their own peace culture and apply their own traditions of peacemaking. Japan has much to offer in this connection.

IKEDA: Again, Japan—because of our past aggression in Asia and our own experience of the horrors of war in places like Okinawa, Hiroshima, and Nagasaki—has the mission and duty to help lead the creation of peace culture. This mission starts with peace education for everyone, regardless of age or nationality.

Children can teach much about peace culture to adults, who often avoid it. In 1992, in Rio de Janeiro, a twelve-year-old girl, Severn Cullis-Suzuki, addressed world leaders assembled at the Earth Summit (formally known as the United Nations Conference on Environment and Development) as follows:

> At school—even in kindergarten—adults teach us children how to behave. You teach us not to fight but to solve problems by talking them over. We should respect other people. We should pick up after ourselves. We should not thoughtlessly hurt other living things. We should try to understand each other and not be greedy. Well then, why do you adults do the very things you forbid us to do? You always say you love us. Well let me say this: If you really do love us, show it in your actions.

This twelve-year-old got a bigger round of applause than anyone else. The heads of state, political and nongovernmental representatives, and other officials rose to their feet applauding with tears in their eyes.

Education As Journey

CONNECTED WITH THE WHOLE WORLD

IKEDA: Education will determine the future of humanity, I have long believed. It is the principle source of light for twenty-first-century society.

BOULDING: In today's world, the human spirit is isolated from the goals it ought to pursue. To change this, education must be connected with the whole planet and all its life forms.

The English word *education* is derived from the Latin verb *educare*, meaning to lead forth. I like to think of education as a leading forth of each individual's special capacities and then a moving on to learn about the human journey on earth and how each of us may participate in it.

IKEDA: This "human journey" calls to mind my first fateful meeting with Toda, who was himself a brilliant educator. It took place during the confused period immediately following World War II, when my peers and I were earnestly discussing and seeking the true meaning of life. The powerful emotions on my first encounter with him (at a Soka Gakkai discussion meeting in 1947) inspired me to compose this impromptu verse:

Traveler,
From whence do you come?
And where do you go?
The moon has set,
But the Sun has not yet risen.
In the chaos of darkness before the dawn
Seeking the light,
I advance
To dispel the dark clouds from my mind
To find a great tree unbowed by the tempest
I emerge from the earth.[1]

To encounter outstanding human beings is in itself a supreme form of education, for such individuals help us cultivate the profound longing to improve ourselves through inquiry and seeking.

BOULDING: The inquiring and seeking spirit is open to learning and the expansion of understanding. Any community that lacks it is impoverished. Today, diminishing contact with others weakens the inquiring spirit. This is very serious.

Beyond Books

IKEDA: It is also a problem in Japanese cities.
Education is not purely a matter of school and family. The whole community must join in the undertaking of education.

Today, however, as we find connections among neighbors growing more tenuous and morality in decline, the educational power of the community as a whole is diminishing. We should all realize that reviving social ties is a global priority for the revival of education.

BOULDING: Today, many urge us to rebuild our communities to enable people to know one another, to care about one another, and to help one another. In this connection, the work of each SGI member makes an important contribution to society.

IKEDA: Thank you for your understanding. The scholar of religion Donald W. Mitchell believes that the SGI has grown into a global organization because it goes beyond individual spiritual revolution and strives for reformation in all aspects of society. A fundamental SGI ideal, again, is being good citizens who contribute to peace, culture, and education. We start by expanding the circle of understanding and friendship through discussion meetings, dialogue, and mutual inspiration among people from all walks of life.

BOULDING: Dialogue is very important to education in the home. My own first step in this direction was to listen to my children from the time they were babies and toddlers right through to now. I am still listening! I have learned so much from them. Children see things that adults overlook, and they understand things on levels that do not occur to adults. Listening to my kids was such a rich experience that some of my early writing was really about what I learned from them.

IKEDA: Your book *Children and Solitude*, which has been translated into Japanese, gives us a good idea of your approach to childrearing. Toynbee once told me that a child's fundamental character is already established by age five.[2] To foster the healthy development of each child, adults should listen to them, engaging them in heart-to-heart exchanges.

Based on your many years of teaching, how do you see education developing in years to come?

BOULDING: Western education is failing on two points. First, there is too much learning indoors in isolation from nature. Second, there is too much book learning. This stance tends to disregard the variety of learning abilities possessed by the human being. Reading is not unimportant, but there are many things to be learned outside books.

IKEDA: Of course, helping students to acquire fundamental knowledge and master basic skills is important. But educators who overemphasize grades and performance, stick to convention, and fail to innovate—while they may succeed in producing so-called good students—cannot cultivate creative individuals. The American philosopher and educator John Dewey believed that social reform depends on schools that can move in new directions, unburdened by poor educational practices of the past. An impasse in education spells stagnation for the entire society.

An educator who had studied in schools practicing Dewey's ideals once told me that the key characteristics of Dewey's philosophy include innovativeness, constant concern with students' best interests, and a focus on self-renewal. Innovative education devoted to student needs—this harmonizes profoundly with the educational ideals we of the SGI strive to realize.

BOULDING: Time and time again in the classroom, I have come to see how important experiential teaching is. In practical undertakings, students always come up with ideas and images that far exceed expectations. Through experiences of this kind, I found teaching rewarding because it was always a process of discovery.

Mental-Physical Balance

IKEDA: The trust you placed in your students must have made them happy and confident, nourishing their development. What were some of your teaching techniques?

BOULDING: For one thing, any course I taught had an experiential component. For example, when I taught "Sociology and the Family," each student was assigned to visit a family at dinnertime to sit at the table and listen and learn from what they heard.

The really important thing is to get out of the classroom and learn from life in the community. I think part of all instruction, from kindergarten to university, should be spent out of doors fostering a sense of symbiosis with nature.

IKEDA: More than seventy years ago, in his book *Education for Creative Living*, Makiguchi pointed out the importance of balancing students' mental and physical lives, proposing the half-day school system. Half of each school day was to be spent doing class work, the other half gaining practical experience in the community.

By the way, many elementary schools in Brazil now incorporate Soka educational ideals to great success. In the past decade, the number of such schools in Brazil has grown to 150.

BOULDING: Your own writing and educational work have revealed to me the spirit of Soka education.

IKEDA: You mentioned developing a sense of symbiosis with nature. To this end, the environment in which an educational institution is located can be vital. Institutions I founded like Soka University of Japan and the Kansai Soka Junior and Senior High Schools are located in natural settings. We strove for a kind of educational environment conducive to training leaders capable of contributing to peace, culture, and education in the twenty-first century. Academic visitors, from home and abroad, have admired our beautiful campuses.

BOULDING: When I was a child, there was a forest near our house. It was a special place for me. In the heart of nature, one is connected with many life forms and is never alone. In such a setting, I clearly understand that the whole earth is a living being of which I am a part. Gaining this understanding is one of the most important parts of education.

Cultivating Seeds

IKEDA: When spring comes, the cherry trees throughout the campus of Soka University of Japan burst into bloom. There is a Chinese proverb that goes: "When planning for a decade, plant trees. When planning for a hundred years, train and educate people."

The many saplings we planted years ago have now become great trees laden with beautiful spring flowers. We pray that our students will grow and flourish as the trees have.

BOULDING: I spent time at the United Nations University during the cherry blossom season and was deeply moved by the lovely flowers. Japanese culture endows its people with the ability to love beauty and to generate tranquil spaces. Just such quiet zones are created in the home, becoming the center of daily life, yet are also connected with everything else. I love this Japanese trait.

IKEDA: I admire your practical approach, always backed up with your actual experience. Education and peace must be part of daily life. Only in planting and nurturing beautiful seeds in the lives of each individual can we see the steady advancement of education and peace. The human revolution that we in the SGI uphold is a down-to-earth, popular movement to sow seeds of peace and happiness in people's lives.

BOULDING: To sum up, the very important idea of sowing and cultivating seeds, which is part of the Buddhist tradition, forms the core of education as *educare*, a leading forth. Education must be more than absorbing learning at a desk. It must be tapping inherent potentialities for the cultivation of humanity in every human being. Accomplishing this requires us to walk cheerfully over the earth, to listen to the spirit in every person, and to grow into our own full humanity.

Women's Inherent Strength

WOMEN IN JAPAN

IKEDA: You and your husband visited Japan on many occasions. When was your first visit?

BOULDING: In the mid-1960s, Kenneth was invited to serve as visiting professor of economics at International Christian University (in Tokyo). I had hoped to make a detailed study of the issue of Japanese women and peace. Kenneth and I were already involved with forming the International Peace Research Association. Coming to Japan, we deepened our friendship with Japanese peace researchers, who were very important in building up the association.

IKEDA: More than forty years ago, around the time the International Peace Research Association was founded, I started writing my novel *The Human Revolution*, which I consider my life's work. Those were dark days. Cold War tensions were high, and war had escalated in Vietnam. Awareness of the duty we all have to generate a tide of world peace motivated me to include the following passage at the beginning of the novel: "Nothing is more barbarous than war. Nothing is more cruel."[1]

BOULDING: You and I share the same attitude toward war.

Kenneth was among the earliest of those who initiated peace research in America,[2] and he devoted the rest of his life to blazing the trail to global peace. News of the bombings of Hiroshima and Nagasaki made me fear that everything we had worked for had crumbled in an instant.

IKEDA: I understand how you felt. In my dialogue with Linus Pauling, *A Lifelong Quest for Peace*, he said that the horrendous bombings of Hiroshima and Nagasaki strengthened his determination to apply his pacifist convictions and strive for an end to warfare—a goal he had once considered unobtainable.[3] Those tragedies remind us of our heavy responsibility for the future of humanity.

What early impressions did Japan make on you?

BOULDING: The first thing I noticed, to my surprise, was that women walked behind men. Still, as I learned from American newspapers, Japanese women were also demonstrating in the streets. How could they do that and still subserviently walk a few paces behind their menfolk? I later learned that the demonstrations were connected with practical domestic affairs, like food and consumption, as well as the need for rebuilding a peaceful society.

IKEDA: Women are often outspoken on matters close to home. For example, in 1918 the women of a fishing village in Toyama

Prefecture, Japan, started the most notable of the so-called Rice Riots. Inflation following the end of World War I had sent prices skyrocketing. The young Zhou Enlai, studying in Japan at the time, thought highly of these protests by ordinary women.

The great strength of women's voices comes from their practical know-how. Their sense of responsibility to protect children, for instance, empowers them to work vigorously for change. Our mutual friend Hazel Henderson launched a campaign against atmospheric pollution because she wanted to protect children. Betty Williams, who won the 1976 Nobel Peace Prize for her efforts in Northern Ireland, described her motivation (speaking at Soka University of America in February 2004) as the desire to preserve a peaceful homeland for children.

BOULDING: The important thing is to develop women's inherent strength and gentleness on a wide scale throughout local communities. As I expanded my contacts on my first visit, I discovered the great intelligence of Japanese women. One, who was very fluent in English, went with me to visit numerous local women's associations, where I had a wonderful time listening to women who were very vocal about their feelings. Because women remained quiet in mixed settings and men did all the talking, I was delighted by these opportunities to understand what women really thought.

IKEDA: Your observation should make Japanese men self-reflect.

EYEWITNESSES AND EDUCATION

BOULDING: It was a great pleasure to observe the quality of those women—their strength, vivacity, and knowledge. I was delighted to write about them as a result of my research.[4]

IKEDA: At the height of the feudalistic Kamakura period (1180–1333), Nichiren made his bold statement that "there should be no discrimination . . . , be they men or women."[5] This is remarkable, given the times in which he lived.

In this spirit, women play central roles in SGI organizations throughout the world.

BOULDING: Women have a tremendous role to play in the local community. But, for long ages, in many countries, not just in Japan, they remained shut up at home with no place in society. That is why the appearance of women stubbornly persisting in peace work in their communities, like those in SGI organizations, is so important.

IKEDA: Our local community is where we build peace and happiness. In this sense, the participation of women in local issues becomes increasingly essential.

BOULDING: I have operated on that premise ever since I got married. When I visited Japan twenty years ago, I learned from Soka Gakkai women about the deeply moving series of wartime recollections they had compiled and published. People without experience of war should be urged to read such books to get an idea of what the victims go through.

IKEDA: The full series, titled *Heiwa e no negai wo komete* (With a Longing for Peace), runs to twenty volumes and includes nearly five hundred invaluable accounts. Women from across Japan volunteered to compile the books, though most of them had no previous experience in publishing or conducting research.[6] An illustrated edition of selections from the series was also produced to serve as a textbook for children.

BOULDING: Memories of war tend to fade. A book of war experiences tailored to the needs of children can play a vital role in peace education by helping keep memories alive.

IKEDA: The creative writing I do is in hopes of cultivating in young minds a sense of peace, justice, and courage. Childhood is the morning of life. What seeds are sown in this time of great sensitivity, what sunlight those seeds receive, what soil surrounds those seeds—these determine the future of each child. These determine the direction society as a whole will move when these children grow up to become agents of social change.

BOULDING: I am convinced that greater interaction in the home is the only way to transcend America's recently intensifying youth problems. Many families today spend practically no time together. Children brought up in such an environment are ill prepared to deal with the conflicts and complexities of today's world. It is lamentable that such children grow up without the influence of an active family life.

IKEDA: The same kind of thing is happening in Japan today. Children experience a safe, reliable harbor only when they can share joys and hardships with their parents.

Soka Gakkai women have led an effort to promote reading aloud to children, as I have mentioned (see Conversation One). Fathers, of course, also need to be involved. I know of an Italian father, an SGI member, who writes stories to share with his children. Ordinarily unable to spend much time with them, he makes a point of nightly storytelling. Nothing makes him happier than seeing his children's eyes sparkle as they listen.

BOULDING: We must expand peace education beyond parent-child relations to communities and all of society. Although children are more sensitive, imaginative, and creative than adults realize, modern society often ignores or looks down on children. I have repeatedly issued warnings on this and worked to develop community peace education in which children play an active role.

THINKING AND LEARNING TOGETHER

IKEDA: How exactly?

BOULDING: For one thing, we involve children in community peace camps and nonviolence training weekends where peace and a caring attitude are cultivated through dialogue. We listen to children. We ask them what they want the world to be like in the future. As becomes obvious from actual experience of this kind, we adults can learn a lot from children. They have imagination. They are full of ideas.

IKEDA: Adults and children should think and learn together about peace.

Makiguchi said it is arrogant for a teacher to urge students to "Be like me." The only kind of model a teacher can set is that of someone striving to develop his or her potential completely. Student and teacher, home and school, should strive together for the goals of happiness in the family and peace in the world.

Proper education cultivates the heart of each member of a community. The depth of this education determines the depth of the community's commitment to peace. Whether we can bring peace culture to full flower in the twenty-first century depends on education.

CONVERSATION TEN

Creating Global Citizens

MUTUAL BONDS

BOULDING: You propose educating people to be citizens of the world. My husband wholeheartedly supported your idea, as I do. As early as the 1980s, you called for a pooling of wisdom to establish a UN Decade of Education for World Citizens and to inspire the United Nations University to engage in education for global citizenship. Those proposals have even greater significance today than they did when they were first advanced.

IKEDA: I treasure the sincere encouragement you and your husband offered the SGI over the years. The Boston Research Center for the 21st Century (renamed the Ikeda Center for Peace, Learning, and Dialogue in 2009), which I founded in 1993, for many years presented a Global Citizen Award to individuals who have made significant contributions to the development of humanity, peace, and education. You were one of the first recipients (in 1996).[1] Presenting it to you was a great honor for us.

BOULDING: I remember that wonderful presentation ceremony clearly. In my thank-you speech, I said that the aim of our peace research and education movement is to help humans live together in a mutually caring and compassionate way. We must deal with our differences and satisfy human needs in ways that harm no one. This means a major reconsideration of our identities, attitudes, values, beliefs, and social skills.

IKEDA: At the awards ceremony, Dr. Kevin Clements praised you as a creator of a network of humanity, a person who has fully realized that rebuilding this sundered world is one of the peacemaker's fundamental roles.

In discussions we held some years back, Norman Cousins told me that, among the many imponderables of the future, one thing is certain: The present generation and all subsequent ones must become citizens of the whole human community.

BOULDING: To accomplish this, we must walk the world reaching out to people and talking with them. In fact, there are unrecognized peacemakers everywhere among us. We have to find them and help them become peacemakers of the future. In this effort, we must not allow the likelihood of persecution to hinder us.

IKEDA: Persecution often only proves that the persecuted are in the right. In a sense, it can be a badge of honor. This is the attitude we of the SGI have taken.

Could you share with me what methods you used as a university teacher to put the peacemaker's faith to work in the classroom?

BOULDING: The important thing is opening spaces for young people, who will be responsible for the future. I have thought a lot about the dynamics of teaching. It needs to be a listening process. In speaking to students in the classroom setting, I was intensely aware of the degree of responsiveness their facial expressions conveyed. In fact, I always try to tune into the people I am talking to so the communication is genuinely two-way.

In any course I taught, I gave students real-life assignments that would give them firsthand opportunities to learn things they couldn't learn from textbooks alone. In courses on international peace studies, for instance, I had students apprentice for the semester with local branches of international NGOs, thus enabling them to discover firsthand how the local connects with the international in a global network of citizens' organizations.

IKEDA: Many people would certainly find your method sound. Direct experience with local and international peace efforts helps qualify young people to be world citizens. The time of youth and adolescence is ideal for cultivating the necessary sensibilities of world citizenship and broadening one's horizons through awareness of other cultures. Shouldn't parents and teachers support young people in this endeavor as much as they can?

BOULDING: We must create more opportunities for children and young people to discover and grow from the amazing diversity of the "ten thousand societies" of the planet.

IKEDA: Direct experience is the best possible education. But reading also contributes to children expanding their horizons and learning the spirit of peace. I have written numerous children's stories to teach them the importance of life, friendship, caring, challenging themselves, and achieving harmonious coexistence with nature.

Television, too, has a role to play in education. I am pleased that a Philippine TV series of twelve of my stories, including *The Cherry Tree* and *The Prince and the Coral Sea*, won an award for most outstanding children's series from the Southeast Asian Foundation for Children's Television (in December 2004). Mag Cruz Hatol, secretary general of the Southeast Asian Foundation for Children's Television, expressed a great awareness of how the excessive violence in today's media makes parents uneasy. It also runs counter to fostering the spirit of peace in young minds.

CHILDREN AND PEACE

BOULDING: By now, there are hundreds of books about how to work with children in developing their peacemaking skills. Many are published by faith groups and by peace organizations, while others appear on the market simply because there is a demand for them. One particularly delightful book is *Peace Quest* by Kelly Gainon. It shows children how to put the abstract idea of peace to use in everyday life. It is a book kids themselves can use.

IKEDA: We can only hope for more outstanding books like that. At the same time, we must give more thought to how adults approach peace education with children. You have already mentioned some of your own practices in this connection.

In 2004, the educators division of the Soka Gakkai agreed on the following mottoes:

All children have innate dignity.
All children brim with the strength to live.
All children are bundles of creativity.
All children are citizens of the world capable of joining heart
to heart.

In many cases, debates on education do not place children themselves at the center. Unfortunately, such debates often overlook them altogether. Adults tend to regard children not as independent personalities but simply as immature beings.

BOULDING: This is something that I feel very strongly about and have written quite a lot about. We always underestimate how much children understand. They understand far more at every age than adults around them think they do. We are always underestimating them. Modern society stifles children's unusual insights and perspectives about what is going on around them.

IKEDA: Children brim with the pristine sensitivity and creativity that many adults sadly seem to have lost. We must remember that—*superior* to adults in many ways—children are the treasures of humanity.

BOULDING: Children can do very creative things for the realization of peace. During the Vietnam War, my oldest son, Russell, who was in high school at the time, helped organize a fast for peace in Ann Arbor, Michigan, where we were living at the time. He and a group of teenagers wore badges that said, "I'm hungry for peace in Selma and Vietnam." They went without food for forty-eight hours. Linking the racial violence in Selma, Alabama, with the military violence in Vietnam, they taught the whole town of Ann Arbor a lesson. And younger children joined them—even some first-graders!

But, in spite of their creativity, children are rarely listened to, let alone encouraged to get involved in peacemaking activities. It is the rare adult who realizes that children sometimes have something to teach grownups!

To help them understand the beauty of the world, as good global citizens must, children's home environments should include elements of play and fun. Children should be taught to enjoy dancing, music, and art; they should learn to love nature and, together with all of us, take part in the great dance of the earth.

CONVERSATION ELEVEN

Women Speaking Out

A Woman President?

IKEDA: In 1987, the World Commission on Environment and Development[1] set forth the important concept of sustainable development. The Commission is also called the Brundtland Commission after its chair, Gro Harlem Brundtland, twice the prime minister of Norway. She was kind enough to send a message for the SGI's exhibition "War and Peace" in Oslo in 1991.

BOULDING: After completing her term as prime minister, she became director-general of the World Health Organization (in 1998). She is a very distinguished and powerful woman and, of course, a fellow Norwegian! I have been deeply impressed by her and have learned a lot from her.

IKEDA: To what political heights can women of her caliber aspire? Do you think a woman will someday be president of the United States?

BOULDING: A woman will eventually be elected president. But that will not be enough. Choosing a new leader does not change everything. Having a woman as president would be only a token if there were not a significant number of women in Congress or in other high offices.

IKEDA: Such a time will and *must* come.

BOULDING: In some countries in the world, women occupy 40 percent of the seats in national governing bodies. As they move into these positions, they bring with them their characteristic ability to listen. I remember Ali Mazrui's rule that a minimum of one-third of the membership of any gathering engaged in important problem-solving activity should be women—a tough criterion not often met.

IKEDA: Actually, since half the world population is female, women should make up half of such organizations. Results are sure to be balanced and reforms sure to proceed in the best way only when political and social movements incorporate women's opinions.

BOULDING: You are a supporter, good! I also think that a woman should be the secretary-general of the United Nations. In fact, one day that will happen.

IKEDA: I think so, too. Margaret Thatcher once shared with me her view that politics is like planting trees for posterity. She said that, since they take a long view of things, women have the greatest concern about the world their children will live in when they grow up.

Corazon Aquino, inheriting the aspirations of her assassinated husband and becoming president of the Philippines with overwhelming popular support, told me that mothers should not discriminate among or try to coerce their children. She looked on herself as the mother of the Philippine people, determined to engender in them respect for truth, justice, and liberty.

As her loving words indicate, leaders must work for the sake of the people. At no time in history have we stood in greater need of leaders—women *and* men—who love the people and devote themselves wholly to the popular good.

Changing the subject a bit, let me ask you about some of the people who have been closest to you.

CARRYING OUT ONE'S MISSION

BOULDING: Certainly my husband was far and away the closest person to me in my life. He was my very best friend.

I have had many other friends. One person I would name is Donella H. Meadows, who participated in writing *The Limits to Growth* for the Club of Rome.

IKEDA: An ecologist, she was well known for her bi-weekly column called "The Global Citizen." The warning for the future that she and others sounded in *The Limits to Growth* echoed throughout the world. In my dialogue with Club of Rome founder Aurelio Peccei (*Before It Is Too Late*), we discussed the environmental problem and many other problems confronting humanity. We agreed that the future of humanity hinges not only on external revolution, like the Industrial Revolution and the technological revolution, but inner revolution—the human revolution.

Another connection I have with the Club of Rome is my friend Ricardo Díez-Hochleitner, a great admirer of Peccei and the club's honorary president, with whom I have also held a dialogue (published as *A Dialogue between East and West*).

BOULDING: Donella and I taught at Dartmouth College at the same time. We saw the world in very similar ways, although our fields were different. She had lots of training in biology and ecology. We meant a lot to each other.

IKEDA: She was also well known for her 1990 article "State of the Village Report" (also known as "Who Lives in the Global Village?"). Its central concept—"If the world were a village of 1,000 people . . ."—was widely adapted on the Internet in the years following September 11, capturing the world's imagination. Using proportional statistics in an easy-to-understand fashion, the report highlighted the rich-poor gap and many other injustices.[2]

BOULDING: She died very suddenly in February 2001. It was a terrible blow.

IKEDA: Hazel Henderson mentioned Donella in *Planetary Citizenship*. I know that you and Hazel, too, have been friends a long time.

BOULDING: I first met her in the 1970s. When one of my sons got married, she opened her house in Princeton, New Jersey, to my kids so they could attend the wedding and have a place to stay.

IKEDA: When I asked whom she respected most, your name came to her lips at once.

BOULDING: Hazel is a self-taught economist and an outspoken woman. She has total self-confidence and inner certainty about what she is doing. Her ability to command an audience has been a great driving force behind the growth of her movement.

IKEDA: She made a deep impression when she reminded me that hope is vital to sustained human growth. This means choosing a path and following it through—carrying out one's mission wherever one is.

RESEARCHING THE LOCAL

BOULDING: Seeing one's chosen path through—this is her way of living.

In long years of research in peace studies and related fields, I have done many studies of women. During our years in Iowa, I came to know Quaker farmers, who have a special quality in their relationship to the soil and the way they organize.

Farm work is very complex and requires great organization. There are so many different things to do. What I had never realized until I met the Iowa Quaker farmers is how much farming women do. They do much more than keep house. In fact, they do much of the actual farm work. I decided it would be a good idea to research the lives of wives on farms and write a report on it.

Doing the research and projects related to it was fun. I enjoyed observing the really remarkable range of things that farm women did, from building fences to making jam and doing woodcarving—to say nothing of cooking and raising children.

IKEDA: Jean-Jacques Rousseau argued that farming is the most fundamental and valuable of human undertakings. Only nations that stress the importance of agriculture deserve to be called truly cultured.

Giving serious thought to agriculture today is, in a sense, to think seriously about our culture. Prizing the environment and valuing life naturally come from this.

Research that sheds light on regional agriculture is sure to become increasingly important. I commend you for developing an interest in farm wives' activities at an early stage of your research.

In this and in your peace studies, what has been your basic approach?

BOULDING: I have always rooted my research work in local communities. Wherever I have lived, I have put down roots in the local community and have made efforts to help people understand that their local groups are part of international networks that also connect directly with the United Nations.

IKEDA: You embody global thought combined with local action. Your research has been carried out in action, not sitting at a desk.

In the age of the Internet, although we can instantly access information from across the globe, what I would call a false image of the world is sadly spreading. There are many things that can be neither seen nor understood unless we make efforts ourselves and pursue dialogue as you have.

BOULDING: I agree entirely. At a study group I attended recently, we discussed the nature of our nonviolence work group and action plans. The important thing is for many kinds of people both to participate in the work of their local communities and to maintain international connections through NGOs and other international groups.

More Than Partnership

A SHARED DEDICATION

IKEDA: A few years back, the late economist John Kenneth Galbraith and I had a series of dialogues on peace, education, and the future course of the global economy. Already ninety-five at the time, Dr. Galbraith radiated a warm humanity and determination to see peace achieved.

BOULDING: Dr. Galbraith and my husband were acquainted through their concern with global issues.

IKEDA: One especially impressive remark Dr. Galbraith made to me revealed both the source of his work for peace and his affection for his family: "My beloved wife, Catherine, and I devote all the strength and intellectual power given us to enabling everyone to live in peace and happiness."

BOULDING: Words reflecting a wonderful relationship.

IKEDA: In 1992, the year before his death, your husband accompanied you to an IPRA conference in Kyoto despite being confined to a wheelchair. A journalist covering the event related to me how, although he had entrusted the struggle to younger people, Kenneth still spoke eloquently for the cause.

What enabled you and your husband to maintain such a harmonious relationship over so long a period?

BOULDING: Our personalities were very different, but we always made room for each other's ways of doing things. Kenneth did things his way, and I did things my way, and we accommodated each other, all within a very deep, shared spiritual life and a basic commitment to world peace.

IKEDA: When two unique personalities come together, emotions and misunderstandings will inevitably come up. But rather than taking those in a negative way, both partners can work to make such differences actually productive for the relationship. Of course, that is not easy. You and your husband succeeded because of the profound trust, beliefs, and ideals you shared.

BOULDING: Sharing a common faith also helped. The word *partnership*, which is sometimes used to describe good husband-wife relationships, is inadequate because our relationship was so much deeper. As I have already said, we first met at a Quaker gathering. The bond between us was born and nurtured by deep faith and a commitment to a peaceful world.

IKEDA: The comradeship you describe reminds me of a floral tribute Madame Deng Yingchao placed on the grave of her husband, Zhou Enlai. The arrangement bore the inscription "Enlai, Comrade in Arms."

No bond is stronger and more beautiful than that of comrades in arms who share life's joys and sorrows. My wife, Kaneko, has accompanied me on my travels around the world to build bridges of friendship and peace. As an expression of my gratitude for her hard work behind the scenes, I wrote her this brief verse: "Walking with you / my indispensable support / as we open the way."

BOULDING: Those words certainly convey the depth of the bond between you two. Sonnets written by my husband are among my personal treasures.

IKEDA: A sensitivity to beauty is the hallmark of humanity. The poetic spirit, proof of our humanity, emerges from deep within us to help us live more richly creative lives.

BOULDING: Kenneth was still writing them in the last months of his life. The sonnets that I read most often now are those from his last years. Each time I read them, I can feel his presence. Through them, he is still part of my life.

A sonnet he wrote for a Quaker wedding is one of my favorites because it so beautifully expresses what being a family means:

Put off the garb of woe, let mourning cease;
Today we celebrate with solemn mirth.
The planting in the ravaged waste of earth

Of one small plot of heaven, a Home of peace,
Where love unfeigned shall rule, and bring increase,
And pure eternal joy shall come to birth
And grow, and flower, that neither drought nor dearth
Shall wither, till the Reaper brings release.
Guard the ground well, for it belongs to God;
Root out the hateful and the bitter weed,
And from the harvest of thy Heart's good seed
The hungry shall be fed, the naked clad,
And love's infection, leaven-like, shall spread
Till all creation feeds from heavenly bread.[1]

IKEDA: In this beautiful and powerful poem, I sense the truth of Tolstoy's belief that poetry is a flame burning in the soul.[2] It has the power to evoke and bring to full flower the good in human beings. Your husband's concept of a "Home of peace," from which eternal joy spreads, sums up the prayers and vows of a noble man. It reveals the brilliance of human life.

BOULDING: I like the sonnet's message about what family means so much that I have read it at the wedding of each of our children. I used the phrase "one small plot of heaven" as the title of a book I wrote about family life.

IKEDA: Reading a poem full of love at a wedding is a wonderful blessing for young people just starting out in life.

TIME MANAGEMENT

IKEDA: Between raising five children, helping your husband in his work, and conducting your research and peace activities, you have led a very busy life. Did you devise any techniques for managing it all?

BOULDING: I do not know exactly how to convey this, but a long time ago I developed a special approach to timing. If you are doing a lot of things and want to be sure each thing gets done when it needs to be done, you have to have a system. Mine is to avoid fretting and maintain a sense of my location in time.

IKEDA: Instead of being at its mercy, you control your own time?

BOULDING: It is more a matter of awareness. First, where am I in the day? Say it is three o'clock in the afternoon now, near teatime. (Kenneth, by the way, always liked his cup of tea at four o'clock.) If I know where I am in the day, I can check what I need to be doing. Then, which day of the week am I in? Today is Tuesday; I must know what things need to be done on this particular day, in this week, and in this month. Where am I in the year? What decade of my life am I in? I ask myself whether I am on target with the different things to be done in relation to each of those time phases.

IKEDA: That gives me a good idea of just how busy you have been. I also think in terms of decades, each with its own goal. I had tuberculosis when I was young, and doctors said I probably would not live to see thirty. So I decided to live life to the fullest. On my thirtieth birthday, I evaluated each decade of my life up to then and started setting goals for the decades to come.

BOULDING: That was a wonderful way to handle your situation.

IKEDA: Given my poor health, every day of my youth was a battle waged in the face of death. But I won out and achieved my goals. I set myself certain challenges, among them writing. Even when I did not feel well, I persevered, page by page.

I kept track of the number of pages I produced each day, each month. My desire to encourage people and advance the cause of peace kept me going. However, after I became a published author, it sometimes took me months to complete a single book.

BOULDING: You persisted in your struggle for decades. I have tried to put into practice the device I just mentioned because periodically I need to stop and relate to the totality of life as a process. As I live in this way, I strive to interconnect myself as a person with my family, my community, my country, the world's countries, and the planet earth itself.

DIRECT CONTACT WITH OTHERS

IKEDA: Connecting in the way you mention gives life its deep meaning. It serves as the foundation for peace, happiness, and value-creation throughout society. In today's often savage society, connections among not only adults but among children are weakening. Humanity is heading toward division rather than unity. Japanese society, too, is becoming warped in this way.

BOULDING: A serious environmental problem in the United States is the lack of local woods where children can play and connect with nature. Often they have only the street or a small yard—if they have anything at all—for a playground. Consequently, they are not connecting with a living natural environment.

When I was a child, we spent a lot of time exploring and playing games in the out-of-doors. Now children spend their time indoors watching television or playing video games, many of which are very violent.

IKEDA: It is important that virtual reality not become the center of children's lives at the expense of their direct contact with nature and other people, thus decreasing their opportunities to sense the value and richness of life. Ralph Waldo Emerson wrote, "[Nature's] light flows into the mind evermore, and we forget its presence."[3] We must restore light to our hearts by opening our minds to nature and our fellow human beings.

BOULDING: Children today are not building community skills the way they do when they get to know their neighborhoods. In a neighborhood, kids understand that different parents expect different things of their children. They learn how different people are.

Families spend much less time together now. We need to rebuild family ties, but this cannot be done in a vacuum. It needs the context of rebuilding neighborhood ties, neighborhood social relationships. This will help strengthen deeper spiritual values for every level of society.

IKEDA: Building a sense of community for children requires, first of all, a revolution in adult awareness. Adults must make more effort to talk to and get to know children in their neighborhood. When children see that many people—not just parents and teachers—are interested in them, care about them, and are willing to discuss things with them, they can grow up healthy and happy.

The Necessity of Vision

IMAGINING REAL OUTCOMES

IKEDA: Makiguchi believed that we must take the long view and have clear goals to actualize in our immediate surroundings. He advocated creating value steadily in daily life.

Your late husband frequently compared the peace culture to a small island afloat on the vast sea of a war culture. But he also thought that this single island of peace would inevitably replicate itself over and over. Secure in this hope, we must persevere as long as there is even the slightest possibility of success. I have devoted many years to the peace movement, and your husband's beliefs accord profoundly with my own.

BOULDING: Up to the present moment, I have steadily worked for the vision Kenneth and I shared. It is important that young people—who must bear the burden of the future—know of his ways of thinking.

IKEDA: You have devoted great effort to awakening a vision of peace in students' minds. How did you come to this?

BOULDING: In the 1960s, at a meeting of economists working on the economic aspects of disarmament, I asked how a totally disarmed world would function. The response was unexpected. They had no idea. They felt their job was to explain the possibility of disarmament. I came to realize that many people working in the peace movement had no clear idea of what a peaceful society would be like. How could they give themselves wholeheartedly to a movement the outcome of which they could not imagine?

IKEDA: No matter how fervid our quest for peace may be, without a clear idea of where *exactly* we are going, there is no way to gather the strength necessary to break through the harsh realities we will face. Our efforts can even lapse into inertia or drift into abstraction.

INDIFFERENCE AND APATHY

BOULDING: The Dutch sociologist Fred Polak was a good friend. He wrote *The Image of the Future* (which later won the Council of Europe Award) while in hiding from Nazi persecution during World War II. Drawing on human history, Polak showed that, no matter how hard times got, societies that believed in their own future repeatedly demonstrated the dynamic power to overcome hardships creatively. But societies that were apathetic and fearful could not generate the energy needed for positive change.

IKEDA: Toynbee said to me, "We must not be defeatist, passive or aloof in our reaction to the current evils that threaten mankind's survival."[1] Polak's argument resonates with Toynbee's. The apathy and indifference evident everywhere in modern society are a huge problem. The SGI's promotion of peace, culture, and education is meant to counteract this apathy in inspiring the desire for reform on a global scale.

For example, many people would prefer to ignore the issue of nuclear weapons. But unless we eradicate this threat, peace remains out of reach. This is why, beginning in the harsh Cold War days of the 1980s, the SGI sounded the alarm as much as possible with our touring exhibitions "Nuclear Arms: Threat to Our World" and "War and Peace." The inspiration for these came from Toda's declaration for the abolition of nuclear weapons, in which he said that, from the Buddhist viewpoint, the existence of nuclear weapons and the threat they pose to humanity's survival are an absolute evil.[2]

INNATE CAPACITY TO CARE

BOULDING: I certainly agree with the SGI belief that a wave of peace can start with the work of individuals. I have long believed that a wholesome, peaceful world is possible if we devote all-out effort to the development of each member of the community. Of course, movements undertaking such a policy may face persecution. But that is no reason to give up.

The SGI policy of giving special attention to the local community is important. Because widespread urbanization deprives them of mutual contacts, many people are calling for the restoration of the local community. Human beings are certainly capable of knowing one another better and caring for and helping one another. In this connection, SGI members are making fine contributions to society by helping each person be a good citizen.

IKEDA: Thank you for your kind and encouraging words. To return to Polak, what was your friendship with him like?

BOULDING: He and his wife lived with us for a year in California to work on a special project dealing with the future. His *Image of the Future* had just been published in the Netherlands (in Dutch), and he had it under his arm when he came to our place in California. Since Norwegian is my native language and I know German well, I asked him if I could try reading it. In preparation, I first read *The Age of Unreason* by Franz Alexander in a "pony": Dutch on one page and English translation on the facing page. By the time I finished the book, I could read the Dutch. With his permission, I translated *Image of the Future* into English, and it became one of the earliest books in the futures movement.[3] Based on Polak's thesis of the importance of "imaging" a positive future in actually bringing about such a future, I then developed a type of workshop for imagining a future world in which there would be no more war. Those workshops are carried on even to this day.

To Define Peace Culture

IKEDA: Your translation of Polak's book stands as a milestone in your peace research.

Speaking of imaging the future, your husband's responses to my annual peace proposals made a strong impression on me. He pointed out that the future is uncertain; it may move in a good or bad direction. But beneath this uncertainty, he found something constant: increasingly stable peace among independent nations, a phenomenon that has been evolving under the radar for more than 150 years.

Your husband mentioned that it started in the Scandinavian countries with the termination of the century-long conflicts among Sweden, Denmark, and Norway. The United States likewise no longer entertains ideas of warring with Canada or Mexico, he went on. And after World War II, the nations of Western Europe, too, have opted for peace. There will be no more wars among England, France, and Germany, he believed, nor will Japan go to war. It is no longer true, he thus concluded, that power comes down to the "power to intimidate."

As he envisioned, we must ensure that the twenty-first century centers not on "hard power" but on the "soft power" of dialogue.

BOULDING: Indeed. And we had better start practicing that in Iraq today! You have set a good example of expanding soft power by visiting countries of different philosophical and cultural backgrounds and establishing bonds among people. You go where the people are, precisely because they are there. In your dialogues, you not only transmit your own ideas to the other party but also listen to what the other party has to say. That is what mutual understanding and bonding are all about.

My own understanding of the term *peace culture* is that it is a culture that promotes peaceable diversity, dealing creatively with the conflicts and differences that appear in every society, because no two humans are alike. It includes lifeways, patterns of belief, values, and behavior. It includes the accompanying institutionalized arrangements that promote mutual caring, well-being, and the equitable sharing of the earth's resources among its members and with all living beings. That is what we are working to achieve for the world we live in.

A World of Progress

THREE DECADES OF PEACE ACTIVISM

IKEDA: This January 26 (2005) marks the thirtieth anniversary of the SGI's birth. Our international organization was formalized in January 1975 on Guam at a conference attended by representatives from fifty-one countries. From that time on, we have consistently promoted peace with ever-renewed determination.

BOULDING: I congratulate you wholeheartedly on this memorable anniversary and am enjoying my own memories of the history of the SGI.

IKEDA: On that 1975 trip, I also visited Los Angeles, New York, Washington, D.C., Chicago, and Honolulu. In New York, I presented to the UN secretary-general a peace petition with ten million signatures collected by the Soka Gakkai youth. The conclusion of my journey was Guam, which, as you know, was the scene of fierce fighting during World War II.

BOULDING: Sending a new message of peace from a scene of tragic war has profound meanings.

IKEDA: I hope so. Today, more than thirty years later, the SGI is active in 192 countries and regions, where, to my supreme joy, our members are fully engaged in their own human revolution while contributing to peace in their local communities.

BOULDING: When I meet with them here in the United States, SGI members always radiate their determination to improve their lives through their faith. They are really a source of hope for the world.

IKEDA: With firm conviction, I told the participants in Guam: "I hope you do not seek after your own praise or glory, but instead dedicate your whole lives to sowing the seeds for the sake of the peace of the whole world. I shall do the same thing."[1]

You and your husband traveled the globe as champions of peace. Which of the many countries you visited made the biggest impression?

TRAVELS FOR PEACE

BOULDING: First of all, I remember India. I traveled there on several occasions in connection with my work as president of the Women's International League for Peace and Freedom (1968–71). And the International Peace Research Association, which I helped found, has close and amicable ties with India. For these reasons and because many of the international organizations I am connected with hold conferences there, I have spent quite some time in India. I have been especially impressed by the rural educational and character-building programs in the so-called Gandhigram (Gandhi Villages), where the aim is to create a classless society on the basis of the teachings of Gandhi's nonviolence movement. Gandhi was a model for humanity. He lived his philosophy, and people came to him and followed his example.

IKEDA: He was a relentless champion affirming through his actions the greatness of nonviolence as a means toward justice. Insisting that what is possible for one person is possible for everyone,[2] he roused the ordinary people and won India's independence.

If strength is defined as moral strength, then women are immeasurably superior to men, said Gandhi. Further, he believed that if nonviolence is the law of our being, the future is with women.[3]

BOULDING: I was greatly impressed by Indian women. The women's movement in India was very strong when I was there. My vice president in the Women's International League for Peace and Freedom was a powerful Indian woman. When she stood up to speak, she could hold a huge crowd in the palm of her hand. She had tremendous powers of expression.

IKEDA: Many women across India are carrying on the Gandhian spirit. One of Gandhi's direct disciples, Dr. Usha Mehta, former director of the Gandhi memorial in Mumbai and a friend of the SGI, is one such champion of nonviolence. She survived four years' unjust imprisonment. Dr. Mehta always remembered how her mentor said that we can build social peace by establishing peace in the minds of women. When this happens, the power of women for peace reaches its full strength and society has no choice but to change.

No one is stronger than a woman fully aware of her mission. The radiance of intelligent, noble women will lead the world.

BOULDING: As I have also said many times, the power of women is what helps move the world. I am certain that more and more women will come to realize that they are the builders of peace culture.

Côte d'Ivoire was a shining example of peace culture. I visited there several decades ago as a participant in a UNESCO conference. Unable to recover from the trauma of colonialism, the country was experiencing horrible poverty and extreme inequality of wealth distribution. Nonetheless, in local communities, the strength to protect and rebuild their peace culture was budding.

IKEDA: In June 1999, I discussed this with Amara Essy, Côte d'Ivoire's foreign minister. His country played a decisive role in the United Nations designating 2000 as the International Year for the Culture of Peace.

As you mentioned, Côte d'Ivoire has sadly suffered from political instability and civil war. I hope that peace and prosperity will come to this country as soon as possible.

Despite such difficult circumstances, Ivorian SGI members work vigorously for peace. For instance, they held their fourth educational seminar there in September 2004. About twelve hundred educators and representatives of other professions held extensive discussions on education and what the future holds for their children.

BOULDING: I am glad to learn of this important undertaking.

IKEDA: I have continually argued for the twenty-first century to be an African century. Because of all they suffered under colonial regimes, the African people deserve the greatest happiness. When I talk with African SGI members, many of whom visit Japan, the powerful radiance in their eyes gives me nothing but hope for the future of their continent.

BOULDING: I fully agree with the idea of the twenty-first century as an African century. I, too, have seen remarkable inner strength in the Africans I have met. Creating peaceful communities in Africa will certainly bring global peace one step closer.

IKEDA: Many nations will have to work together for the sake of African peace and development and, by extension, the future of humankind. Cooperation is essential. As an old Ivorian maxim has it, "A grain of rice cannot be grasped with a single finger."

BOULDING: Another country that has impressed me is my own native land: Norway. As I have already said, I was born there but moved to America at the age of three. Years later, I made a trip along the northern coast of Norway to Sámiland, where many Sámi still lead creative and self-sufficient lifestyles under the demanding conditions of the far north.

As might be expected, I still feel connected to my homeland.

SOURCES OF VITALITY

IKEDA: Norway has great appeal worldwide. What do you find most attractive about the United States?

BOULDING: I love that America is a melding of peoples from everywhere. My wish for the future is more feedback within and between local communities. In our own town, Needham, Massachusetts, we protest the Iraq war every Saturday afternoon in front of the town hall. Participants come from various sectors of the community and from local interfaith groups. We need more networks among communities.

IKEDA: I, too, see America's cultural and ethnic diversity as a great source of its youthful vitality and appeal. Can the United States put these characteristics to use in creating an ideal community for the new age?

BOULDING: Well, there is a long way to go! To achieve it, there need to be councils at all levels—local, state, regional, national, and international—facilitating creative solutions that enable people of different races, cultures, and income levels to work together to build a more sustainable, friendly, peaceful world. For another thing, I should like for America's future to be free of the military and of profit-oriented corporations.

No single nation should lead others. In the different kind of world emerging, nation-states will no longer play the roles they play now.

IKEDA: In terms of future development, what countries do you find most promising?

BOULDING: Spain and Norway are good examples of the way nations may develop in the twenty-first century. Spain is actually a federation of provinces. While working with UNESCO in Spain, I attended conferences in Barcelona and spent some time in Catalonia, which has a very strong anti-military and utopian tradition: Nobody has power over anybody else.

IKEDA: The great cellist Pablo Casals, who deeply loved his native Catalonia, was famous for opposing Nazism and the Franco dictatorship. Until his death at ninety-six, he struggled relentlessly against racial and ideological discrimination. The Catalan traits you point out may account for his indomitable personality.

HONORING DIVERSITY

BOULDING: I see every country in the Europe of the future as simply a federation of tribal groups. As in Catalonia, any group that wants to use its own ethnic language in teaching could do so with authorization from the European Union.

If all Europe is seen as a proliferation of ethnic and tribal groups with languages and histories of their own, with many migrating between countries and regions, the European Union must certainly honor this diversity. Unfortunately, today's Europe is having great difficulty in accepting this migration—as is the United States.

IKEDA: When the time you describe arrives, all regions and ethnic groups within the greater European framework will recognize and respect one another's diversity. Europe should move in the direction of such harmonious symbiosis in the future. Indeed, in recent times, many European cities have been cooperating on a regional level transcending national boundaries.

BOULDING: Members of the European Union have a long struggle ahead in learning to respect diversity. French and English will not remain the dominant languages. And think of the challenges in Asia and Africa! But we humans can and will learn to live together as a family on this planet. There is a spirit in each of us that will make this possible. First, though, we must learn to listen to that spirit and to listen to one another.

IKEDA: Most important is a universal, shared philosophy to connect diverse people in harmony. Surely what we need today to counter egoism and nationalism is an awareness of ourselves as global citizens. This is the ideal consistently advocated by Toda.

Prevailing conditions may sometimes make it difficult for us to be optimistic about the future. However, as Count Richard Coudenhove-Kalergi, the father of the European Union, said in his dialogue with me, to triumph over pessimism demands optimistic action. No matter how dim the outlook, we should work to open the path toward peace and hope, changing people's pessimism into optimism through courageous action. It is my sincerest hope and determination that you and I can together continue our efforts for the sake of peace.

The Two-hundred-year Present

The Andalusian Example

IKEDA: Some thirty years ago, I asked Toynbee what historical period and place he would most like to have been born in. He replied Xinjiang (now the Xinjiang Uyghur Autonomous Region of China) soon after the start of the Common Era, because Central Asia at that time was a meeting point for Buddhist, Indian, Greek, Iranian, and Chinese cultures. How would you answer the same question?

BOULDING: I am drawn to many historical periods but for a long time have been especially fascinated by Andalusia, Spain, in the fourteenth century, when Arab culture was arriving and coming into contact with the culture of the Roman Empire. Several great forces came together. Though the period was not free of conflict, the Arab court culture of Andalusia witnessed a great philosophical and scientific flowering.

IKEDA: You previously mentioned Spain as a model twenty-first-century society (see Conversation Fourteen). So Spain also interests you as a place of historic encounters among civilizations. In the period you mention, students from across Europe went to study at the Islamic universities of Andalusia.

BOULDING: People from all areas of society came together and were constantly engaged in lively discussion. New participants from various ethnic groups joined in to learn one another's languages and engage in dialogue, which they chose in preference to warfare. This cultural situation lasted until the appearance of Ferdinand II and Isabella I in the fifteenth century.

IKEDA: They united Spain and completed the *reconquista*, or reconquest, of the Iberian Peninsula by destroying the Moorish kingdom of Granada in 1492.

BOULDING: Up until that time, Spain had a vigorous culture from which we have inherited a great deal of our intellectual wealth. I would have found it very exciting to live then and to witness how discussion propelled things along.

IKEDA: In our global age, the fourteenth-century Andalusian spirit of dialogue and tolerance has much to teach us about avoiding cultural standardization and maintaining our individual identities while still stimulating and influencing one another.

You have said, again, that peace culture is not just a way of resolving conflicts—it is a way of creatively managing differences. Defined in this way, a peace culture can be said to have existed in Islamic Andalusia. The theory of the clash of civilizations paints a picture of self-contained, isolated development, but civilizations grow and develop through ceaseless exchange, mutual stimulation, and unending dialogue.

BOULDING: In Europe and North America, history has been taught as a series of civilizations, culminating in Western civilization as the pinnacle. This very false picture suggests that all other civilizations are merely a buildup to the civilization of the West. Actually, however, long predating even literacy in Europe, ancient civilizations in Asia, the Middle East, and Africa produced sacred writings and great documents about humanity, art, music, and so on. Western civilization does not become an important actor on the world stage until recent times.

IKEDA: Several thinkers, including Franz Fanon, Edward Said, and Gayatri Chakravorty Spivak, have penetratingly analyzed and, in fact, criticized the West-centric view of history. But their views are still far from the mainstream in the nations forming the core of today's world order. As Said points out in *Orientalism*, the West-centric approach is more than a philosophy of history—it seeks control over non-Western politics, economics, culture, and education. This worldview is interrelated with the widening gap between rich and poor, the loss of cultural diversity, and other related problems generated by globalization.

BOULDING: I want children growing up in all countries—especially in the United States—to realize that they are recipients of the wisdom many civilizations have evolved over thousands of years. It is terribly important for people in the West to understand how much harm colonialism did by imposing cultural boundaries. In addition, they must understand the integrity of other peoples who have their own languages, histories, and cultural achievements. Understanding that the 191 nation-states on earth embody "ten thousand societies," we must encourage respect for the incredible diversity of human creativity.

IKEDA: Transcending national boundaries and the narrow nationalism that separates people must begin with research into, as you describe, the incredible diversity of human creativity and education that respects that diversity. The Austria-born philosopher Ivan Illich had some interesting things to say on this topic. First, he believed that the meaning of the word *peace* differs depending on the age and culture. For example, the meanings of the Latin *pax*, Hebrew *shalom*, and Hindi *shanti* all differ slightly. Illich believed that we need a history of peace, which would undoubtedly be much richer and more complex than our history of war, and that a history consisting of nothing but conflict oversimplifies the past.

BOULDING: In a book I wrote titled *Cultures of Peace, the Hidden Side of History* (2000), I argued that history is thought of as the history of war, when actually true human history describes how people have coped with the various issues that came their way. Although some interactions were violent, far more were nonviolent. But this rarely appears in history books. We need a new approach to history because too many people believe that humans are basically war-making animals and that the more weapons we have, the safer we are.

IKEDA: The belief that humans are fundamentally warlike inevitably becomes justification for war and violence. This notion itself inflames the cycle of hatred and violence, thus spreading mistrust and prejudice among people.

Buddhism regards violence as a manifestation of the destructive impulse within human life. Although it cannot be entirely eliminated, this impulse can be controlled. I am convinced that we have the wisdom to adjust and alter our social systems to prevent violent outbreaks.

Exactly as you say, it is dangerous to conclude that human history is synonymous with a record of war. Several writers, including Erich Neumann in *The Great Mother*, Marija Gimbutas in *Goddesses and Gods of Old Europe*, and Riane Eisler in *The Chalice and the Blade: Our History, Our Future*, have clearly identified war-free periods of history. For instance, a matriarchal, peace-loving society flourished in Neolithic Europe but was replaced by a patriarchal culture when, in the Bronze Age, Proto-Indo-Europeans invaded and the spread of Indo-European languages began.

BOULDING: We need to tell the women's story. When men go to war, women and children are left at home. European history shows that hospitals were originated by women as ways of organizing care both for children and the wounded. Women created institutions and schools because they had the time to teach their children. Since they were home and were not off fighting wars, women, especially nuns, developed educational systems and hospitals in the midst of wartime. Instead of always just describing how the Crusaders battled all the way to Constantinople and the Holy Land, it would be very interesting to write a history of the Crusades from the perspective of women.

ORDINARY PEOPLE AS LEADERS

IKEDA: The Crusaders offer a striking example of how the meaning of history changes vastly depending on how you interpret events. No doubt the Crusades would look very different from the standpoint of women.

Toda insisted that truly studying history entails developing your own perspective on it. He instructed me to always view history from the standpoint of ordinary people. The simple fact that war has caused the greatest suffering to ordinary people enrages me. History is certainly much more than the exploits and triumphs of heroes.

BOULDING: From time to time, social movements generate eloquent leaders like Gandhi or King. But what is really important is that social movements develop in ordinary people a new awareness of what the world can be like. Great religious figures like Abraham, Mohammed, Jesus, and Shakyamuni ultimately articulated new forms of popular understanding that emerged in their times.

IKEDA: The lives of nonviolent heroes like Gandhi and King suggest superhuman courage and leadership abilities. Both of them, however, continually emphasized the mission of each and every individual.

This was Shakyamuni's message, too, as is clear from the "Expedient Means" chapter of the Lotus Sutra, where he states his goal to "make all persons equal to me, without any distinction between us."[1] Everyone is endowed with limitless wisdom, courage, and good fortune, he believed. His intent was to develop these qualities in all his disciples to the degree to which he himself had manifested them. In India, Buddhism died out largely because it started to set Shakyamuni apart as someone special, someone isolated from ordinary people.

BOULDING: Too often, leaders with great charisma have seized power. I am interested in social movements that enable leaders to emerge who, while still charismatic, do not grab power.

As an example, when Norway was invaded during World War II, you could say no charismatic leaders emerged. Instead, a widespread resistance movement created a complete, silent system of underground communication and self-governance. Nobody needed to make loud declarations.

The movement arose from interpersonal relationships that evolved during the Nazi occupation. Of course, this had a lot to do with qualities inherent in Norwegian society. They are the qualities of sharing responsibility, being responsible for one another, and not seeking to be the spokesperson or the leader.

Change comes from creative movements by the people. In a creative society, spokespersons, no matter how eloquent, are not power-grabbers of the kind that can very quickly lead society astray.

ALL EQUALLY WORTHY

IKEDA: History and our own times, too, offer examples of movements—religious and political—that have, after starting as social reformations embodying popular hopes, become authoritarian, ossified, and alienated from ordinary people. In contrast to such movements, the SGI remains and must forever remain a great hope for the people. To maintain this, we rely on the mentor-disciple relationship.

When a movement imagines it can assume absolute, inviolable authority, it has stagnated. Then, though some of the original ideals may linger, the movement no longer has the vibrant power to realize them.

Some people incorrectly interpret the mentor-disciple relationship as one of formalized superiority and submission. But, according to the Buddhist teachings, this should not be the case.

The Buddhist philosophy that *all are equally worthy of respect* is no abstract doctrine. It must become the core of one's own way of life.

To truly achieve this in Buddhist practice, the disciple needs a mentor who is both a great teacher and a fellow pursuer of self-improvement. Herein lies the true mentor-disciple way. In the simplest terms, it is a relationship of equality between companions who share the will for self-improvement.

BOULDING: The sharing is very important. With members in many countries, the SGI can make truly important contributions to the international peace community. In addition, because of the spiritual depth it helps provide, the SGI's peace movement is more than political in nature. An exclusively political peace movement cannot attain the stage of mutual inspiration essential to pacifist efforts. Similarly, we Quakers, too, work as a peace-creating spiritual community across national borders.

IKEDA: Always on behalf of the ordinary people, I am determined in the coming years to uphold the voice of ethics, the power of culture, and the spirit of innovation in education.

As our dialogue draws to its conclusion, may I ask you to send one more message to young people working for peace in the twenty-first century?

BOULDING: I think in terms of what I call the two-hundred-year present when considering ways in which humanity can approach the ideal of being true global citizens. The two hundred years consist of the century that has passed since the birth of people who are one hundred today and the century that will pass before infants born today are centenarians.

We have and will come into contact with people living through those two centuries across the planet. Each person, from the oldest to the youngest, is part of a greater community. Our contact with them means that we do not live in the present only. If the present moment were all, its occurrences would crush us. But if we think of ourselves as existing in a greater span of time—the two-hundred-year present—what a multitude of partners each of us will have in our particular lifetime, from youth to old age!

IKEDA: A profound, thought-provoking idea. Buddhism teaches:

> If you want to understand the causes that existed in the past, look at the results as they are manifested in the present. And if you want to understand what results will be manifested in the future, look at the causes that exist in the present.[2]

A brilliant future begins here and now with our first bold step forward. I hope that you and I can continue to work together to expand a network of friendship in years to come. By devoting ourselves completely to the cause of peace, we can make recompense to the victims of past wars and create a world in which the people of tomorrow indeed live in happiness.

Peace Culture: The Problem of Managing Human Difference

An article by Elise Boulding from the Summer 1998 issue of Cross-Currents.

The creative management of differences is at the core of peace culture; in other words, it is not a culture without conflict. Since every human individual is different from every other, conflict is a basic part of any social order. Each of us sees, hears, and experiences the world uniquely, and we spend our lives bridging the differences between our perceptions (and the needs and wishes they generate) and the perceptions of others. Even though it is reasonable to ask why we do not fight constantly, given our differences, much of the time we do this work peacefully. The explanation lies in the two opposing needs for bonding and autonomy. Every human being needs to bond with others. We need to be part of a community; we need others to care for us; we need to care for others. Children who do not experience this caring have trouble dealing with others throughout their lives. At the same time, we need autonomy, our own space—room enough to express our individuality.

A peace culture maintains creative balance among bonding, community closeness, and the need for separate spaces. It can be defined as a mosaic of identities, attitudes, values, beliefs, and patterns that leads people to live nurturingly with one another and the earth itself without the aid of structured power differentials, to deal creatively with their differences, and to share their resources. Although peace cultures exist as separate, identifiable societies, they are not common. They may be found among some, but not all, indigenous peoples and in faith-based communities totally committed to nonviolence. Purely aggressive cultures, in which everyone is actively defending his/her own space at the expense of others' needs, also exist; they are not common either. Usually, we find coexisting clusters of peaceableness and aggression. Each society develops its own pattern of balancing the needs for bonding and autonomy.

The balance may change over time with periods of more peaceable behavior following periods of more violent behavior. It cannot be said that humans are innately peaceful or aggressive. Both capacities are there. It is socialization, the process by which society rears its children and shapes the attitudes and behaviors of its members of all ages, that determines how peacefully or violently individuals and institutions handle the problems that all human communities face in the daily work of maintaining themselves.

We might think of problem-solving behavior as a continuum. At one end lies war in its various forms: extermination of the other, limited war, threat systems, and deterrence. One then comes to arbitration, mediation, negotiation (exchange), and mutual adaptation. Toward the far end from war is cooperation, integration, and, at the greatest remove from extermination, union. Understanding the wide range of alternative approaches to conflict in this way can help to clarify choices.

The Culture of Peace

Because religious traditions and teachings are important shapers of societies, it is important to identify two contrasting themes in religions: holy war culture and holy peace culture. The holy war culture is a male-warrior construct based on the exercise of power. Often headed by a patriarchal warrior God, it typically demands the subjection of women, children, and the weak to men, the proto-patriarchs. The social structure of patriarchy continues to mold generations of the major religious traditions—Hinduism, Buddhism, Judaism, Christianity, and Islam.

In the holy peace culture, by contrast, love is the prime mover of all behavior. It is a gift from the Creator, or Creative Principle. Women and men share with one another, as brothers and sisters, each person equal to every other. The weak are cared for and troublemakers reconciled. Nonviolent holy peace communities do exist as minority presences in the major religious traditions. In Christianity, there are the Anabaptists, and in Islam, Sufis—to mention only two—but they are minorities.

The holy war culture has tended to encourage the exercise of force at every level, from family to international relations. The holy peace culture might work to restrain the use of force, but historically its voice has often been muted. This century has been characterized by rising, increasingly intrastate, violence that has left little room for the workings of a peace culture. In fact, globally, society is out of balance.

This situation need not be permanent, however. Each society contains in itself resources that can help to shift the balance from a preoccupation with violence toward peaceful problem-solving behavior. These include a perennial, utopian longing for peace, both secular and faith-based peace movements, environmental and alternative-development movements, and women's culture.

A utopian longing for peace shows up in the variety of visions of the Isles of the Blessed, Paradise, and similar havens of delight that inhabit every human tradition. It is remarkable that even the most war-like people can imagine gentle and peaceful ways of living. This ability to imagine a better way of life never disappears. When other social conditions permit, these images of a different future can empower social change movements and produce a new dynamic toward nonviolence.

The holy peace teachings of each religious tradition have generated peace movements over the centuries and continue to do so today. Christian peace fellowships—Catholic, Orthodox, and Protestant—increasingly collaborate with Jewish, Muslim, Hindu, and Buddhist peace groups in interfaith efforts to bring an end to all forms of violence, including war. Their strategies to develop the spiritual awareness of humankind as one family include intensive nonviolence training in local communities and political efforts to delegitimate militarism and support peaceful diplomacy.

Secular peace movements have been multiplying as part of a larger twentieth-century social phenomenon: There has been an encouraging emergence of international NGOs that provide linkages among people's organizations with common social, economic, political, and cultural interests. There are now some twenty thousand such organizations. While the number of NGOs actively dedicated to peace building is modest, the majority of NGOs contribute, to some degree, to the development of an international peace culture because their common concern is human betterment. Their effect is multiplied by the fact that they provide an interface between local householders and communities with otherwise remote regional and national governmental bodies. They also provide means of communication with the United Nations and other inter-governmental agencies to facilitate problem solving and conflict resolution, and circumvent rigid governmental bureaucracies.

Today, peace-movement NGOs are building new coalitions to work for the abolition of nuclear weapons by the year 2000 as a step toward general disarmament. Their work is substantially amplified by those scientists and professionals whose work is focused on peace and disarmament. The Pugwash Conference on Science and World Affairs (named for the place in Canada where the group first met in the 1950s) is the oldest and most prestigious group of scientists trying to develop ways of controlling militarism; it has made notable contributions to each of the more limited arms-control agreements that have been achieved so far. The International Association of Physicians for Prevention of Nuclear War, the International Association of Lawyers Against Nuclear Arms, Economists Against the Arms Race, and the new Center for Economic Conversion (in Bonn, Germany) are resource organizations invaluable to the work of peace activists. The International Peace Research Association has played a special role in recent decades in providing policy-oriented research on peace processes and in developing peace-studies programs in universities around the world to train student generations in nonmilitary approaches to international and civil conflicts.

A new set of professional organizations focused on practitioner skills of conflict resolution, mediation, and reconciliation is just beginning to form international NGO networks and to establish peace-building training centers on each continent. Another important development of recent decades has been the creation of NGOs to maintain peace teams on the Gandhian model of the Shanti Sena (Peace Army). Peace Brigades International has been the pioneer, and many secular and faith-based NGOs now support their own peace teams.

Women's organizations are an important part of the peace movement. Recent examples include the Women's International League for Peace and Freedom's "Great Peace Journey" to heads of state around the world; the women's peace camps established at military bases such as Greenham Common in England; the Women for a Meaningful Summit Group that permits no "big power" summit to take place unquestioned; and the relatively new WEDO, the Women's Environment and Development Organization. The series of UN women's conferences is slowly creating a general awareness of the need for the knowledge, skills, and competence of women in the conflict-ridden arena of public decision-making. The international women's movement has also raised public consciousness about the relationship between violence against women, in homes and in communities, and war itself.

Children and youth are all too often ignored in peace-movement activity, but their own initiatives are beginning to have public impact; the Voice of Children and Rescue Mission Planet Earth are two such organizations. At the 1995 World Summit for Children in San Francisco, young delegates drafted an impressive proposal for a UN Youth Assembly. This proposal is still under consideration in the UN system.

The environmental movement's close relationship to the peace movement and the concept of peace culture is evident in the Earth Charter initiative, developed since the UN Conference on Environment and Development at Rio. A document to be signed by peoples everywhere (to be accepted, it is hoped, by the UN General Assembly in 2000), it spells out a commitment by humanity to exist in peace with all living things—living sustainably, sharing resources equitably, and resolving conflicts nonviolently. The Earth Charter also gives a special role to the "ten thousand societies"—ethnic, racial, and cultural-identity groups that straddle national borders—in the creation of a culture of peace, drawing on their many time-tested but unrecognized ways of settling disputes peacefully. Overlapping with these groups are the many thousands of grassroots organizations that apply their resources and ingenuity to the creative resolution of local environmental, economic, and social crises. The Chipko "hugging the trees" movement is an example of how such nonviolent action can work—in this case saving forests from a destruction that would also impoverish local populations. The structural violence of a globalized economy run by megacorporations can be countered nonviolently through local self-help organs, such as the Grameen Bank, which assists in pooling local resources to empower the productive capacity of villagers.

All of these movements are helping to create an interconnected but diverse mosaic of peaceful lifeways and a new sense of planetary identity in opposition to the global military system that sucks up common resources to maintain the dominion of powerful states and divides the rich from the poor.

WHERE PEACE CULTURE CAN BE FOUND

The familial household is an important source of peace culture in any society. It is there that women's nurturing culture flourishes. Traditionally, women have been the farmers as well as the bearers and rearers of children, the feeders and healers of the extended family. The kind of responsiveness to growing things—plants, animals, babies—that women have had to learn for the human species to survive is central to the development of peaceful behavior.

Through most of human history, people have lived in rural settings and in small-scale societies. Just as each familial household develops its own problem-solving behavior, so each social group has developed strategies of conflict resolution rooted in local culture and passed on from generation to generation. Similarly, each society has its own fund of adaptability, built on knowledge of local environment and the historical memory of times of crisis and change. Such knowledge and experience are transmitted through familial households as they are organized into communities. The knowledge is woven into religious teachings, ceremonies, and celebrations; it is present in women's culture, in the world of work and the world of play, in environmental lore, in the songs and stories of each people. These are the hidden peace-building strengths of every society.

The familial household can also be the source of violence. Exercise of power in the patriarchal family model too often leads to wife abuse and child abuse. Boys can be gentled by their experience of growing up male when the values of nurturing and sharing exist in the community and women are visible and equal participants in the more public life of the society. If we look at societies that set a high value on nonaggression and noncompetitiveness, and therefore handle conflicts by nonviolent means, we can see how certain distinctive child-rearing patterns produce nurturing adult behavior.

The Twa people in northeastern Zaire (now the Democratic Republic of the Congo), now endangered by the civil war that has swept over their country, provide a striking example of how a peaceful society raises its children. The Twa are hunter-gatherers who dwell in the rain forest. The basis for their peacefulness is their relationship to the rain forest, which is mother, father, teacher, and womb. The family hut is also a symbolic womb. Children grow up listening to the trees, learning to climb them at an early age so that they can sit high in their branches. Twa is a listening culture, but also a singing and dancing culture, as adults and children sing to and dance with the trees. *Ekima*, quietness, is highly valued over *akami*, disturbance.

Although this preference for quietness and harmony is reinforced at every stage of life, it does not preclude children's rough-and-tumble play. There is also a lot of petty squabbling among adults, which tends to be controlled by ridicule. While children are slapped when they engage in forbidden activities and nuisance behavior, they are also taught interdependence and cooperation. Adults seem to enjoy horseplay and noisy disputes. Semi-humorous "sex wars," in which men and women line up for tugs-of-war, serve as tension-dissipaters; they break up with much laughter. They are also an indication of the companionable equality between women and men. Most groups have a "clown" whose antics also help to keep conflicts from getting out of hand. For all of the squabbling, disagreements rarely get serious.

The contrast between the love of forest silence on one hand and the raucous pattern of argument, joking, and ridicule on the other is interesting. The Twa place a high value on "letting it all hang out"; they do not let conflicts fester. In this culture, there seems to be a nature-based equilibrium based on a combination of listening, singing, dancing, and squabbling that is not easy for Westerners to understand.

Another example of unusual child-rearing practices in a peaceful society is found among the Inuit. Living in the circumpolar North, from eastern Siberia through Greenland and Canada to Alaska, they survive the harsh and unforgiving winter cold through cooperation and social warmth. Violence and aggression are under strong social prohibition. The social values are centered on: (1) *isuma*, which involves rationality, impulse control, careful problem-solving, and foresight; and (2) *nallik*, which is love, nurturing, protectiveness, concern for others' welfare, and suppression of hostility.

The distinctive child-rearing practices that produce these rational, compassionate, controlled adults revolve around what Jean Briggs, an anthropologist who has studied the Inuit, calls *benevolent aggression*. This behavior combines an unusual combination of warm affection for infants with a complex form of teasing that creates real fear in children and then induces them to laugh at their fears. The title of one of Briggs' studies, "Why Don't You Kill Your Baby Brother?," suggests the extremes to which the teasing goes, at least from a Western perspective. That this behavior produces adults who exhibit both *isuma* and *nallik* (and a remarkably peaceful society) I would ascribe to the fact that young children in general are far more socially perceptive and far more sophisticated in their assessment of social situations than adults usually give them credit for. They can figure out what is going on and learn to respond creatively when given the chance. Although one can imagine this tricky form of socialization going wrong with some individuals, it does seem to turn children into self-reliant problem solvers with a well-developed sense of humor, who are affectionate and acutely aware of the disciplined anger-control systems in themselves and others. Girls and boys get the same type of socialization, and Inuit men and women are equally resourceful. They like to fondle infants and baby arctic animals, share food communally, and laugh together. The skill of handling conflict playfully, as in song duels (or drum matches) between offended parties, produces enjoyable public events instead of battles.

The Anabaptist cultures of the historic peace churches, originating in Europe in the late Middle Ages in revolt against the power structures of church and state, live on today in a number of religious communities, among which the best known are the Mennonites, the Brethren, and the Quakers. These communities share with the peaceful societies described above a careful attention to rearing children to become peaceful adults. While each group has its own unique practices, they all live "in the world but not of it," holding to testimonies of simplicity, gender and racial equality, and personal and social nonviolence. In war, they refuse military service; their commitment is rather to work for the realization of "the peaceable kingdom." The cultivation of the divine seed in each child makes child-rearing and family life of central importance. Girls and boys are reared in similar ways and are prepared early for participation in decision-making. Explicit training in nonviolent responses to conflict and alternative ways of dealing with conflict are emphasized. At their best, these Anabaptist communities produce adults with imagination and skill in organizing peace-building projects for social betterment.

Celebrations are the play life of a society, and a healthy play life strengthens the peaceableness of any people by reaffirming the best in their social values. Feasting and gift-giving emphasize sharing and reciprocity, the sense of the community as one family. When sharing and gift-giving have a character of spontaneity and exuberance—and singing and dancing are freely and widely practiced—then celebration is a powerful reinforcer of peaceful and caring community relations. It becomes an opportunity to let go of grudges, a time of reconciliation among persons whose relations may have become strained. To the extent that there is a clearly articulated basis for the celebration, patterned in ritual, it can also become a way of reconnecting with creation itself, a reminder of the oneness of the cosmos and of all living things. Celebration becomes a time for the making of vows in service to the community; it marks the rites of passage from birth to death, wounding and healing, beginnings and endings, and historical moments from the remembered past.

When celebrations lose their playfulness, when gift-giving becomes carefully calibrated exchange, when performances become competitive, then these rituals lose their replenishing character and cease to be resources of genuine peaceableness. Play itself, by its very nature, performs a serious creative function for each community. Taking place outside of the realm of everyday life, play nonetheless creates boundaries, rules, and roles ("let's play house—you be the daddy and I'll be the mommy"), and structures spaces in which children can create their own realities. Play can also teach nonviolence and self-control when, for example, in the rough-and-tumble of play a child is inadvertently hurt.

That play space is also where children can practice grown-up activities does not take away from the fact that play is done *for its own sake,* "for fun." Playing can therefore be important for adults as well. Although competitive sports may work against the spontaneity of play for both players and spectators, the rudiments of play survive.

There are other less obvious forms of play. Some are highly developed: the mind at play in science; the muse at play in poetry, music, and art; the body at play in song, dance, and drama. Play goes on at the grassroots level in the folk culture of each society, and it goes on among the elites, although the play of each tends to take separate forms in terms of style, language, and content. Some art and some sports have become so violent that they have lost the character of play. The recovery of play as fun, a basic heritage of every society, is the best response to such violence.

Zones of Peace

As far back as the historical record goes, we know of sanctuaries, or safe places, for anyone under threat. Temples and holy sites have become sanctuaries; sometimes the land immediately around a king's palace has been designated as safe for persons fleeing their enemies. Marketplaces have always been treated as zones of peace, since violence would destroy trading activities. Both the Hebrew Bible and the Koran declare croplands and orchards, as well as the women and children who tend them, protected in time of war. The Catholic Church extended this protection through the Pax Dei to pilgrims, merchants, and cattle in the twelfth century, and controlled the violence of war by forbidding soldiers to fight on certain days of the week.

Since the beginning of the nuclear age, there have been many grassroots movements to persuade states or regions to declare themselves nuclear-weapon-free zones, and counterpart movements to define individual towns and cities as zones of peace. This combination of traditional sanctuary practice with new peace-movement activity has resulted in a gradual spread of physical areas that have a certain political and social commitment to peace culture.

Today there are twenty-three or twenty-four states that have renounced military defense and have no armies. There are also a growing number of regions that have been declared nuclear-weapon-free zones by a treaty process facilitated by the United Nations and signed by the member states of the region. The treaties of the Antarctic (the Antarctic Treaty System), the Treaty of Tlatelolco (Latin America), the Treaty of Raratonga (the Asian Pacific), and most recently the treaties of Bangkok (Southeast Asia) and Pelindaba (Africa) all identify these areas as nuclear-weapon-free zones. Clearly, this is a direction in which states would like to go, although the major powers often do their best to hinder this treaty process. The production and transport of materials for nuclear weapons are specifically forbidden in these treaties in all of the states in the regions. Intergovernmental bodies monitor compliance. Peace NGOs in each region have played an important role in getting states to sign these treaties and to uphold them. Outer space and the seabed are also in theory nuclear-weapon-free areas, although they are not so in practice, mainly because the major powers insist on preserving freedom of movement for nuclear materials on the seas and in space.

Indigenous peoples on all continents seek zones of peace for their territories. The World Council of Indigenous Peoples, the Inuit Circumpolar Conference, the International Indian Treaty Council, and the Unrepresented Nations and Peoples Organization all seek removal of weapons and environmentally damaging activities from their territories, annually bringing new cases before relevant UN bodies.

None of these treaties or zones of peace would have come into being without intensive activity by local NGOs. At the grassroots level, both NGOs and community-based organizations have succeeded in declaring more than five thousand towns and cities around the world nuclear-free, or more strongly, zones of peace. Once such a declaration has been officially made, there are all kinds of opportunities for creative community action. Boulder, Colorado, and Cambridge, Massachusetts, are two such communities. Both have active nonviolence training and mediation programs in the communities and school systems. Sister city projects link local communities in different world regions. Local projects include economic conversion of military plants, environmental protection (particularly from toxic wastes), and local-to-local international trade (with a strong emphasis on human and social development and the infrastructure needed to sustain such development). They also include developing peace education and conflict resolution programs in schools, creating peace parks and public peace sites, and planting peace trees. Local members of the International Federation of Sister Cities, the international program of the National League of Cities, the World Congress of Local Authorities, and other NGOs help both with local community education and with the international networking process. As a result, many cities and some state governments have established international affairs offices and have declared "peace policies."

The declaration by local churches and citizens' organizations of violence-free zones in the midst of some of the major metropolises of the Americas and Europe is one more manifestation of this growing international movement. Courageous community groups in war-torn areas from Somalia and Bosnia/Croatia to the Philippines have made pacts with soldiers, guerillas, and rebels to keep their localities free of weapons and fighting.

Another aspect of the zone-of-peace movement can be found in UNESCO's World Cultural and International Heritage Sites. The Zone of Peace Foundation is promoting an expansion of these sites to include more places of sanctuary, refuge, and peace building in such public arenas as museums and schools around the world. Special national environments that need protection—waters, forests, mountains, grasslands—are also included. A feature of all of these zone-of-peace sites is that local managers are to develop training programs in conflict resolution so that visitors will not only experience a violence-free setting but can learn the skills of peacemaking. The Global Land Authority for the Development of Peace Zones has actually put peace-building initiatives in place in such conflict areas as Cyprus and the Kuriles. Probably the most experienced peace builders and protectors of zones of peace are groups like Peace Brigades International and other civilian teams skilled in nonviolent response to conflict and threat.

The United Nations works through many vehicles in the building of zones of peace beyond the UN-facilitated treaties already mentioned. These include UN peacekeeping (which only works when peacekeeping forces have special training), UN observer teams and police forces, and the activities of UN agencies, especially UNESCO and UNICEF. An important "new" concept from UNICEF is the declaration of each child to be a zone of peace, which can provide the basis for a number of creative initiatives involving not only protection of children but more active peace training in schools. The 1990 UN World Summit for Children began this process. One important outcome of that gathering is an ongoing Children's World Summit, through which children and youth are working to create a UN Youth Assembly. Children are an important but largely ignored resource in the development of peace culture.

THE FUTURE OF PEACE CULTURE

In this exploration of peace culture, we have considered the fact that peace, like war, is a social invention. We have noted the sometimes precarious balance between humans' need for bonding and autonomy. If humans did nothing but bond with one another, societies would be dull, lacking in adventure. If they did nothing but claim individual space, societies would be full of action, but it would be aggressive and violent action. Finding the right balance in a complex world in which technology shields us from one another and even from ourselves is difficult. Global corporations weaken local economic and social capacity. The military-industrial system seems beyond the ability of states to control, and the biosphere is losing its capacity to regenerate itself and feed the growing population of humans. Weakened local community and family systems are racked by violence.

How can peace culture grow and flourish, bring us better futures, under such conditions? We have noted the persistence of social images of life at peace, the ineradicable longing for that peace, and the numbers of social movements working for a more just and peaceful world. With the growth of the global civil society in this century, there are linkage systems among peoples and movements that never before existed, making possible unheard-of interfaces between governmental and nongovernmental bodies. We have seen that there are many sites where peace learning can take place, from family and community to international peace-building centers, and noted peaceful micro-societies like the Twa, the Inuit, and the Anabaptist communities. We have seen that the zone-of-peace concept is spreading.

It seems that in spite of the visibility of violence and war, many are able to see past that violence to a different future world. People who cannot imagine peace will not know how to work for it. Those who can imagine it are using that same imagination to devise practices and strategies that will render war obsolete. The importance of the imagination cannot be overestimated.

Peace culture, however, is not just a figment of the imagination. It exists in daily life and habitual interaction as people get on with their lives and work, negotiating differences rather than engaging in interminable battles over just how to solve each problem as it comes up. Aggressive posturing slows down problem solving. Violence is more visible and gets more attention in our history books and in our media than peace does. But peace culture will take us where we want to go.

Kenneth Boulding always used to say, "What exists is possible." Since peace culture exists in all the social spaces described here, it is possible. If we want the world to be one planetary zone of peace, full of adventure and the excitement of dealing with diversity and difference, without violence, humans can make it so.

Peace and Human Security: A Buddhist Perspective for the Twenty-first Century

A speech by Daisaku Ikeda at the University of Hawaii's Spark M. Matsunaga Institute for Peace, East-West Center, Honolulu, Hawaii, January 26, 1995.

Hawaii draws all people into the beautiful embrace of her nature. East and West meet here in friendship; diverse cultures mix and blend in harmony; there is a balance and fusion of the traditional and the modern. It is therefore an especially appropriate place to consider the issues of peace and security, issues of fundamental importance to humankind.

I myself began my travels to the world here in Hawaii in 1960, the year that this Center was established. My earnest desire since youth had been to help bring forth a brilliant dawn of global peace from here in Hawaii, stage of the tragic outbreak of the Pacific War, initiated by militarist Japan.

Looking back, we can say that the twentieth century has been stained by the all too common slaughter of humanity at human hands. Our century has been termed a century of war and revolution; aptly so, for with two world wars and countless revolutions, it has been an unprecedented and bloody torrent of conflict and upheaval.

Advances in science and technology have produced a dramatic increase in the lethality of our weapons; it has been estimated that a hundred million people died violent deaths during the first half of this century. Under the Cold War regime that followed, and since then, regional and internal conflicts have claimed more than twenty million lives.

At the same time, the income gap between the Northern and Southern hemispheres continues to grow, with some eight hundred million people living in hunger. We cannot turn a blind eye to the structural violence by which tens of thousands of precious young lives are lost daily to malnutrition and disease.[1]

Furthermore, many thinkers point with alarm to the spiritual impoverishment, rampant in both East and West, that demonstrates the vacuity of mere material prosperity.

What has twentieth-century humanity gained at the cost of this staggering sacrifice of human life? As we approach the end of this century amid deepening disorder, no one can suppress a sense of anguish at this question.

I am reminded of the following passage from the Lotus Sutra, which contains the essence of Mahayana Buddhism:

> There is no safety in the threefold world;
> it is like a burning house,
> replete with a multitude of sufferings,
> truly to be feared, . . .[2]

This passage gives voice to an unrestrained empathy for humanity, tormented by the flames of suffering and terror.

In the same sutra, his gaze fixed on this agonized panorama,

Shakyamuni Buddha makes the following declaration: "I should rescue them from their sufferings and give them the joy of the measureless and boundless buddha wisdom so that they may find their enjoyment in that."[3]

This determination is seminal in the thinking of Buddhism; from it flows a tradition of dynamic action toward the creation of an indestructible realm of security and comfort amid the stark realities of society. The foundation for this endeavor is always the inner reformation of the individual and the resultant renewal and invigoration of life and daily living. My mentor, second Soka Gakkai president Josei Toda, termed this "human revolution."

Under the sway of the nineteenth-century cult of progress, we have feverishly devoted ourselves in this century to enhancing the structures of society and the state, laboring under the delusion that this alone is the path to human happiness. But to the extent that we have skirted the fundamental issue of how to reform and revitalize individual human beings, our most conscientious efforts for peace and happiness have produced just the opposite result. This, I feel, is the central lesson of the twentieth century.

I was greatly encouraged by the fact that East-West Center President Michel Oksenberg, a noted authority on security issues, holds similar views on this subject. When we met in Tokyo last autumn (October 1994), he expressed himself thus: "If people live in a spiritual void, they will experience insecurity. They will not know stability. They will not feel at ease. The nations and states in which they live will therefore not be offering their people true security. Real security requires that we consider not just the security of the state but that we also include in our considerations the security of cultures and individual human beings."

Our task is to establish a firm inner world, a robust sense of self that will not be swayed or shaken by the most trying circumstances or pressing adversity. Only when our efforts to reform society have as their point of departure the reformation of the inner life—human revolution—will they lead us with certainty to a world of lasting peace and true human security.

With this as my major premise, I would like to offer some ideas regarding three transformations that we face on our way toward the twenty-first century: from knowledge to wisdom; from uniformity to diversity; and finally, what I would term from national to human sovereignty.

From Knowledge to Wisdom

The first transformation I would like to discuss is the need to move away from our present emphasis on knowledge toward a new emphasis on wisdom. Piercing to the heart of the matter, Toda stated that confusing knowledge for wisdom is the principal error in the thinking of modern man.

Clearly, the volume of information and knowledge possessed by humanity has undergone an extraordinary increase compared to a hundred or even fifty years ago. It can hardly be said, however, that this knowledge has led to the kind of wisdom that gives rise to human happiness. Rather, the suffering generated by the grotesque imbalance between our knowledge and our wisdom is succinctly symbolized by the fact that the most sublime fruits of our science and technology have been nuclear weapons and the widening North-South development gap to which I referred moments ago.

With the advent of an increasingly knowledge-and-information-based society, it becomes all the more crucial that we develop the wisdom to master these vast resources of knowledge and information. The same communication technologies that can be used to incite terror and hatred in whole populations, for example, could just as easily produce a dramatic expansion of educational opportunity worldwide. The difference lies solely in the degree and depth of human wisdom and compassion.

The consistent intent of Buddhism is to develop the compassionate wisdom that is inherent in the depths of human life. Nichiren wrote the following in a letter to one of his disciples: "Your practice of the Buddhist teachings will not relieve you of the sufferings of birth and death in the least unless you perceive the true nature of your life. If you seek enlightenment outside yourself, then your performing even ten thousand practices and ten thousand good deeds will be in vain. It is like the case of a poor man who spends night and day counting his neighbor's wealth but gains not even half a coin."[4]

A distinctive characteristic of Buddhism, and of Eastern thought in general, is the insistence that all intellectual activity be developed in intimate dialogue with such existential, subjective questions as "What is the self?" and "What is the best way to live?" The passage I quoted is representative of this style of reasoning.

There is growing concern that competition for water and other natural resources will be an increasingly frequent cause of regional conflicts. In this connection, I am reminded of the wisdom that Shakyamuni demonstrated in response to a communal conflict over water in his native state.

When his peripatetic teaching brought Shakyamuni back to Kapilavastu (where he had grown up), he found that a drought had depleted the waters of a river running between two ethnic groups in the region, bringing them into conflict. Neither group was prepared to yield; both had taken up arms and bloodshed seemed unavoidable.[5]

Stepping between the two factions, Shakyamuni admonished them: "Look at those who fight, ready to kill! Fear arises from taking up arms and preparing to strike."[6]

It is precisely because you are armed that you feel fear—this clear and simple reasoning reverberated in the hearts of the conflicting parties, awakening them to the folly of their actions. Everyone put down their weapons, and friend and enemy sat down together.

When Shakyamuni spoke again, he addressed not the rights and wrongs of the immediate conflict but the primal terror of death. He spoke with power and intimacy on overcoming the foremost fear—of our own inevitable death—and on living a life of peace and security.

Of course, compared to the fierce complexity of contemporary conflicts, this episode may appear all too simplistic in its outcome. The present war in the former Yugoslavia, to take but one example, has roots that reach back nearly two thousand years. During that time, the region has seen the schism between the eastern and western Christian churches, the conquests of the Ottoman Turks and, in this century, the atrocities of fascism and communism. The tangled animosities of race and religion are indescribably deep and powerful. Each group emphasizes its uniqueness; each group knows and draws upon its history for justification. The result is the deadly stalemate we see today.

It is for just these reasons that I find an urgent meaning in the pattern demonstrated by Shakyamuni's courageous dialogue. Our times demand an embracing wisdom that, rather than dividing, brings into view that which we share and hold in common as human beings.

The teachings of Buddhism offer a treasure trove of peace-oriented wisdom. Nichiren, for example, offers this pointed insight into the relationship between the basic negative tendencies within human life and the most pressing external threats to peace and security: "In a country where the three poisons [of greed, anger, and foolishness] prevail to such a degree, how can there be peace and stability? . . . Famine occurs as a result of greed, pestilence as a result of foolishness, and warfare as a result of anger."[7]

The wisdom of Buddhism enables us to break the confines of the lesser self, the private and isolated self held prisoner by its own desires, passions, and hatreds. It further enables us to contextualize the deep-rooted psychology of collective identity as we expand our lives, overflowing with exuberance, toward the greater self, which is coexistent with the living essence of the universe.

This wisdom is not to be sought in some distant place but can be found within ourselves, beneath our very feet, as it were. It resides in the living microcosm within and wells forth in limitless profusion when we devote ourselves to courageous and compassionate action for the sake of humanity, society, and the future. Through this kind of bodhisattva practice, we develop the wisdom to sever the shackles of ego, and the spheres of our disparate knowledge will begin to turn with vibrant balance toward a prosperous human future.

FROM UNIFORMITY TO DIVERSITY

The second transformation I would like to discuss is from uniformity to diversity. I deeply appreciate having the opportunity to discuss this theme here—in Hawaii, these "rainbow islands" that are a veritable symbol of diversity—and now, as we begin the UN Year for Tolerance (1995).

The citizens of Hawaii are truly at the forefront of humanity in their efforts to harmonize and draw forth unity from diversity, and this will continue to be an issue of singular importance as we move into the future. Your invaluable pioneering endeavors can, I believe, be likened to the *ohia* tree, which is the first to sink its roots into the barrenness of recent lava flows and sends forth lovely deep-red blossoms.

As exemplified by modes of economic development that aim exclusively at the maximization of profit, modern civilization tends to the elimination of difference—the subordination of both natural and human diversity to the pursuit of monolithic objectives. The result of this process is the grievous global *problématique* that confronts us today, of which environmental degradation is but one aspect. It is vital that we pursue a path of sustainable human development based on a profound sense of solidarity with future generations. A new appreciation of human, social, and natural diversity is, in a sense, an inevitable reaction to the present crisis.

I am reminded of the wisdom of Rachel Carson, marine biologist and pioneer of the environmental movement. In 1963, one year before her death, she expressed her views in this way: "Now I truly believe that we in this generation must come to terms with nature, and I think we're challenged, as mankind has never been challenged before, to prove our maturity and our mastery, not of nature but of ourselves."[8]

The increasing attention focused on the Pacific Rim relates in no small way, I am convinced, to the hope that this "experimental sea," characterized by such remarkable ethnic, linguistic, and cultural diversity, will play a leading role in bringing together the human family.

Hawaii is the crossroads of the Pacific and has a rich history of peaceful coexistence—accepting the contributions of many cultures and encouraging the mutual appreciation of diverse values. As such, I am convinced that Hawaii will continue to be a pioneering model for the emerging Pan-Pacific civilization.

The wisdom of Buddhism can also shed considerable light on the question of diversity. Because one central tenet of Buddhism is that universal value must be sought within the life of the individual, it works fundamentally to counter any attempt to enforce uniformity or standardization.

In the teachings of Nichiren we find the passage "The cherry, the plum, the peach, the damson . . . without undergoing any change."⁹ This passage confirms that there is no need for everyone to become "cherries" or "plums" but that each should manifest the unique brilliance of his or her own character.

This simile points to a fundamental principle of appreciation for diversity that applies equally to human beings and to social and natural environments. As the concept of "revealing one's intrinsic nature" indicates, the prime mission of Buddhism is to enable all of us to blossom to the fullest of our potential. The fulfillment of the individual, however, cannot be realized in conflict with or at the expense of others but only through active appreciation of uniqueness and difference, for these are the varied hues that together blossom into the flower gardens of life.

Nichiren's teachings also contain the following imagery: "It is like the situation when one faces a mirror and makes a bow of obeisance: the image in the mirror likewise makes a bow of obeisance to oneself."¹⁰ I think this beautifully expresses the all-encompassing causality that is the heart of Buddhism. The respect we demonstrate for the lives of others returns to us, with mirrorlike certainty, ennobling our lives.

The Buddhist principle of dependent origination reflects a cosmology in which all human and natural phenomena come into existence within a matrix of interrelatedness. Thus we are urged to respect the uniqueness of each existence, which supports and nourishes all within the larger, living whole.

What distinguishes the Buddhist view of interdependence is that it is based on a direct, intuitive apprehension of the cosmic life immanent in all phenomena. Therefore, Buddhism unequivocally rejects all forms of violence as an assault on the harmony that underlies and binds the web of being.

The following words of Professor Anthony Marsella of the University of Hawaii are an excellent summation of the essence of dependent origination: "I intend to accept and to embrace the self-evident truth that the very life force that is within me is the same life force that moves, propels, and governs the universe itself, and because of this I must approach life with a new sense of awe, humbled by the mystery of this truth, yet elated and confident by its consequences. I am alive! I am part of life!"[11]

By focusing on the deepest and most universal dimensions of life, we can extend a natural empathy toward life in its infinite diversity. It is the failure of empathy, as that great pioneer of peace studies Johan Galtung notes, that in the end makes violence possible.

Professor Galtung and I are engaged in preparing a dialogue for publication (*Choose Peace*, 1995). One subject of our discussion has been the education of children and youth and the need to instill a spirit of positive engagement with those whose very difference and "otherness" can extend and enrich us. This kind of open-ended empathy enables us to view human diversity as a catalyst for creativity, the basis of a civilization of inclusion and mutual prosperity.

I would like to note in passing that the SGI's efforts to promote cultural exchange and interaction around the world are based on this conviction and determination.

FROM NATIONAL TO HUMAN SOVEREIGNTY

The third transformation I would like to discuss is from national to human sovereignty. Undeniably, sovereign states and issues of national sovereignty have been the prime actors in much of the war and violence of the twentieth century. Modern wars, waged as the legitimate exercise of state sovereignty, have involved entire populations willy-nilly in untold tragedy and suffering. The

League of Nations and later the United Nations, each founded in the bitter aftermath of global conflict, were in a sense attempts to create an overarching system that would restrain and temper state sovereignty. We must acknowledge, however, that this bold project today remains far from the realization of its original aims. The United Nations approaches its fiftieth anniversary (1996) laden with a trying array of problems.

It is my belief that, if it is to become a true "parliament of humanity," the United Nations must base itself on the so-called soft power of consensus and agreement reached through dialogue, and that the enhancement of its functions must be accompanied by a shift away from traditional, military-centered conceptualizations of security. As one suggestion, through the creation of a new environment and development security council, the United Nations would be empowered to engage the pressing questions of human security with renewed energy and focus.

In this effort, it is essential that we effect a paradigm shift from national to human sovereignty—an idea expressed powerfully by the words "We the peoples . . . ," with which the UN Charter opens. Concretely, we must promote the kind of grassroots education that will foster world citizens committed to the shared welfare of humanity, and we must foster solidarity among them.

As an NGO, the SGI is engaged in developing effective activities on a global scale, focusing particularly on youth, to inform and raise the awareness of the world's citizens surrounding the unique opportunity presented by the fiftieth anniversary of the United Nations' founding.

From the viewpoint of Buddhism, the transformation from state to human sovereignty comes down to the question of how to develop the resources of character that can bravely challenge and wisely temper the seemingly overwhelming powers of official authority.

In the course of our dialogues held some twenty years ago, Toynbee defined nationalism as a religion, the worship of the collective power of human communities. This definition applies equally, I feel, to both sovereign states and to the kind of nationalism that, in its more tribal manifestations, is fomenting regional and subnational conflicts throughout the world today. Toynbee further required that any future world religion be capable of countering fanatical nationalism as well as "the evils that are serious present threats to human survival."[12] In particular, I am unable to forget the profound expectation that Toynbee expressed with regard to Buddhism, which he termed "a universal system of laws of life."[13]

Indeed, Buddhism possesses a rich tradition of transcending secular authority and making it relative through appeals to, and reliance on, inner moral law. For example, when Shakyamuni was asked by a Brahman named Sela to become a king of kings, a chief of men, Shakyamuni replied that he was already a king, a king of the supreme truth.

Equally striking is the drama of Shakyamuni halting the plans of the imperial state of Magadha to exterminate the Vajjian republics. In the presence of the minister of Magadha, who had come with brazen intent to inform Shakyamuni of the planned invasion, Shakyamuni asked his disciple seven questions about the Vajjians. With some elaboration, these are:

1. Do they (the Vajjians) value discussion and dialogue?
2. Do they value cooperation and solidarity?
3. Do they value laws and traditions?
4. Do they respect their elders?
5. Do they respect children and women?
6. Do they respect religion and spirituality?

7. Do they value people of culture and learning, whether they be Vajjian or not? Are they open to such influences from abroad?

The answer to each of these questions was "yes." Shakyamuni then explained to the minister of Magadha that so long as the Vajjians continue to observe these principles, they will prosper and not decline. Thus, he explained, it will be impossible to conquer them.

These are the famous "seven principles preventing decline," the seven guidelines by which communities prosper, expounded by Shakyamuni during his last travels.[14]

It is interesting to note the parallels with contemporary efforts to establish security not through military might but through the promotion of democracy, social development, and human rights. This incident is also a vivid portrait of Shakyamuni's dignity and stature as a king of the supreme truth addressing secular authority.

It was in this same spirit that Nichiren issued his famous treatise "On Establishing the Correct Teaching for the Peace of the Land" in 1260, directed at the highest authorities in Japan at that time, admonishing them for remaining deaf to the cries of the people. From that time on, Nichiren's life was a series of unending, often life-threatening persecutions. He, however, expressed his sense of inner freedom in this way: "Even if it seems that, because I was born in the ruler's domain, I follow him in my actions, I will never follow him in my heart"[15]; and elsewhere, "I pray that before anything else I can guide and lead the ruler and those others who persecuted me"[16]; and also, "When one practices the Lotus Sutra under such circumstances, difficulties will arise, and these are to be looked on as 'peaceful' practices."[17]

Relying on the eternal Law within to rise above the sway of evanescent authority in pursuit of nonviolence and humanity—

it is in the course of this grand struggle that one experiences an indestructible life-condition of comfort and security. I am further confident that these declarations of soaring human dignity will resound strongly and deeply in the hearts of world citizens as they create the global civilization of the twenty-first century.

The three transformations I have outlined come together in the process of human revolution, the reformation of the inner life, its expansion toward and merger with the greater self of wisdom, compassion, and courage. It is my firm conviction that a fundamental revolution in the life of a single individual can give rise to the kind of consciousness and solidarity that will free humanity from its millennial cycles of warfare and violence.

During World War II, first Soka Gakkai president Tsunesaburo Makiguchi engaged in a spirited confrontation with the military authorities of Japan. Even in prison, and until his death there at age seventy-three, he pursued principled debate, leading several among those who had judged and jailed him to appreciate and even take faith in Buddhism.

Seeking to live up to that spiritual inheritance, I began my own dialogue with the world's citizens here in Hawaii thirty-five years ago. It is my determination to devote the rest of my life to the endeavor, which I hope I will share with you, of marshalling the manifest wisdom of peace to create a new era of hope and security in the coming century.

In closing, I would like to share the following words of Gandhi, whose lifetime devotion to the themes we have discussed today has long inspired my profound affection and respect: "You have to stand against the whole world although you may have to stand alone. You have to stare the world in the face although the world may look at you with bloodshot eyes. Do not fear. Trust that little thing in you which resides in the heart."[18]

Notes

Conversation One

1. As of publication, some 790,000 people have viewed the exhibition "Women and the Culture of Peace" in a total of twenty-seven cities.

2. In 1983, Daisaku Ikeda began writing peace proposals to the United Nations, which he has continued to publish annually on the January 26 anniversary of the founding of the Soka Gakkai International. These proposals offer perspectives on critical issues facing humanity, suggesting solutions and responses grounded in Ikeda's Buddhist humanism. They also put forth specific agendas for strengthening the United Nations, including avenues for the involvement of civil society.

3. Hazel Henderson and Daisaku Ikeda, *Planetary Citizenship: Your Values, Beliefs, and Actions Can Shape a Sustainable World* (Santa Monica, CA: Middleway Press, 2004), pp. 133–53.

4. *The Writings of Nichiren Daishonin*, vol. I (Tokyo: Soka Gakkai, 1999), p. 385.

Conversation Two

1. *The Lotus Sutra and Its Opening and Closing Sutras*, trans. Burton Watson (Tokyo: Soka Gakkai, 2009), pp. 221–28.
2. *The Book of Kindred Sayings (Samyutta Nikaya)*, ed. and trans. F.L. Woodward, 5 volumes (London: The Pali Text Society, 1922), 1:2
3. Rabindranath Tagore, *The English Writings of Rabindranath Tagore*, vol. 4 (New Delhi: Atlantic Publishers & Distributors, 2007), p. 433.
4. For a discussion of the source of this phrase, see: http://lightand silence.org/2007/02/walk_cheerfully_over_the_world_1.html.
5. Nichiren, *The Record of the Orally Transmitted Teachings* (Tokyo: Soka Gakkai, 2004), p. 165.
6. Soka schools: As of publication, there are fourteen institutions ranging from kindergartens to universities in Japan, Brazil, the United States, South Korea, Singapore, Malaysia, and Hong Kong.

Conversation Three

1. Soka education: The ideals of Soka (value-creating) education that serve as the foundation of the Soka school system have their origin in the philosophy and concerns of Tsunesaburo Makiguchi, a school principal, educational philosopher, and founder of the Soka Gakkai. Soka education aims to foster the innate creativity and unique potential of students and to develop their capacity for independent thought and for lifelong, self-motivated learning and development.
2. Officially called the Declaration of Principles on Interim Self-Government Arrangements, the Oslo Accords of 1993 set forth a framework for future relations between the Israeli government and the Palestinian Authority. Initially a cause for optimism, the Accords dissolved over the years, amid ongoing chaos and violence.
3. *The Writings of Nichiren Daishonin*, vol. I, p. 579.

4. Daisaku Ikeda, *A New Humanism: The University Addresses of Daisaku Ikeda* (New York and Tokyo: Weatherhill, Inc., 1996), p. 155.

CONVERSATION FOUR

1. Also known as the Mukden Incident or the September 18 Incident (especially in China). It represented an early event in the Second Sino-Japanese War, although full-scale war would not start until 1937. On September 18, 1931, near Mukden (now Shenyang) in southern Manchuria, a section of railroad owned by Japan's South Manchuria Railway was dynamited. The Imperial Japanese Army, accusing Chinese dissidents of the act, responded with the invasion of Manchuria, leading to the establishment of Manchukuo the following year.

CONVERSATION FIVE

1. The Mystic Law is another name for the Law of Nam-myoho-renge-kyo, which is seen in Nichiren Buddhism as the universal law or principle. Nam-myoho-renge-kyo literally means devotion to Myoho-renge-kyo, which is the Japanese reading of the Chinese title of the Lotus Sutra.
2. NGO: *nongovernmental organization* refers to a legally constituted association with no participation or representation of any government, sometimes defined as a civil society organization.
3. Elise Boulding, "Peace Culture: The Problem of Managing Human Difference," *CrossCurrents*, Summer 1998, vol. 48, Issue 4.
4. Peace Constitution: The Constitution of Japan is sometimes referred to as the Peace Constitution because of its renunciation of the right to wage war, as stated in Article 9: *"Aspiring sincerely to an international peace based on justice and order, the Japanese people forever renounce war as a sovereign right of the nation and the threat or use of force as means of settling international disputes.*

(2) To accomplish the aim of the preceding paragraph, land, sea, and air forces, as well as other war potential, will never be maintained. The right of belligerency of the state will not be recognized."

CONVERSATION SIX

1. Elise Boulding and Kenneth E. Boulding, *The Future: Images and Processes* (Thousand Oaks, CA: Sage Publications, Inc., 1995), p. 144.
2. Ibid.
3. The phrase "ten thousand societies" is used by Elise Boulding, as well as by some anthropologists, to loosely signify the diverse cultures of the indigenous people of the world. These cultures predate our national boundaries and identities. In Dr. Boulding's view, these cultures provide a possible foundation for efforts to create peace cultures in the modern world. See Elise Boulding, *Cultures of Peace: The Hidden Side of History* (Syracuse, NY: Syracuse University Press, 2000).
4. Arnold Toynbee and Daisaku Ikeda, *Choose Life: A Dialogue* (London & New York: I.B. Tauris & Co., 2007), p. 51.

CONVERSATION EIGHT

1. Daisaku Ikeda, *The Human Revolution*, book 1 (Santa Monica, CA: World Tribune Press, 2004), p. 233.
2. *Choose Life: A Dialogue*, pp. 99–100.

CONVERSATION NINE

1. *The Human Revolution*, book 1, p. 3.
2. Kenneth Boulding published *The Economics of Peace* in 1945, one of the first publications to focus on peace research. He was involved in establishing the Center for Research on Conflict Resolu-

tion at the University of Michigan in 1957, the first such center at a U.S. university.

3. Linus Pauling and Daisaku Ikeda, *A Lifelong Quest for Peace: A Dialogue* (London & New York: I.B. Tauris & Co., 2009), pp. 63–64.

4. Elise Boulding, "Japanese Women Look at Society," *The Japan Christian Quarterly*, January 1966.

5. *The Writings of Nichiren Daishonin*, vol. I, p. 385.

6. In 1986, Kodansha International published an English edition consisting of selected translations from the series under the title *Women against War*.

CONVERSATION TEN

1. From 1995–98, the Boston Research Center for the 21st Century (renamed the Ikeda Center for Peace, Learning, and Dialogue in 2009) presented a Global Citizen Award to leaders who had contributed globally in such fields as peace, human rights, education, and the environment.

CONVERSATION ELEVEN

1. Also known as the Brundtland Commission after its chair Gro Harlem Brundtland, it was convened by the UN General Assembly in 1983 to address growing concern "about the accelerating deterioration of the human environment and natural resources and the consequences of that deterioration for economic and social development."

2. After the publication of her article, Meadows' statistics were adapted for use in a popular poster that was distributed at the 1992 Earth Summit in Rio de Janeiro. Over the years, the statistics have also been cited or adapted on the Internet, usually describing the world as a village of 100 people (as opposed to 1,000). It is estimated that millions of people have viewed these emails and Web

pages. Additionally, Meadows' concept has been incorporated into a great variety of lessons and curriculum plans.

CONVERSATION TWELVE

1. Elise Boulding, *One Small Plot of Heaven: Reflections on Family Life by a Quaker Sociologist* (Wallingford, Pennsylvania: Pendle Hill Publications, 1989), p. 1.
2. *The Cambridge Companion to Tolstoy*, ed. Donna Tussing Orwin (Cambridge, UK: Cambridge University Press, 2002), p. 14.
3. Ralph Waldo Emerson, *Nature*, in *Essays and Lectures*, ed. Joel Porte (New York: Library of America, 1983), p. 23.

CONVERSATION THIRTEEN

1. *Choose Life: A Dialogue*, p. 45.
2. Second Soka Gakkai president Jōsei Toda made his historic declaration calling for the abolition of nuclear weapons on September 8, 1957, at a meeting of 50,000 members of the Soka Gakkai's youth division at Mitsuzawa Stadium, Yokohama, Japan. His stance was that nuclear weapons and their use must be absolutely condemned, not from the standpoint of ideology, nationality, or ethnic identity but from the universal dimension of humanity and our inalienable right to live.
3. Futures studies is the philosophy, science, art and practice of postulating possible, probable, and preferable futures and the worldviews and myths that underlie them. Also known as futurology.

CONVERSATION FOURTEEN

1. *A Lasting Peace: Collected Addresses of Daisaku Ikeda*, vol. I (New York and Tokyo: Weatherhill, Inc., 1981), pp. 162–63.

2. Mahatma Gandhi, *All Men Are Brothers* (New York: Continuum, 2005), p. 4.
3. Ibid., p. 162

Conversation Fifteen

1. *The Lotus Sutra and Its Opening and Closing Sutras*, p. 70.
2. *The Writings of Nichiren Daishonin*, vol. I, p. 279.

Appendix Two

1. See Johan Galtung, *Peace and Development in the Pacific Hemisphere* (Honolulu: University of Hawaii Institute for Peace, 1989).
2. *The Lotus Sutra and Its Opening and Closing Sutras*, p. 105.
3. Ibid., p. 95.
4. *The Writings of Nichiren Daishonin*, vol. I, p. 3.
5. See V. Fausboll, ed., *The Jataka*, vol. 5 (London: Luzac and Company, Ltd., 1963), p. 412; H. Smith, *Sutta-Nipata Commentary II Being Paramatthajotika II*, 2 (London: Curzon Press, 1966), p. 566.
6. See "Attadanda Sutta," *The Suttanipata*, trans. H. Saddhatissa (London: Curzon Press, 1987), p. 109; Anderson, Dines, and Helmer Smith, *Suttanipata* (London: Routledge & Kegan Paul), p. 182.
7. *The Writings of Nichiren Daishonin*, vol. I, p. 989.
8. Paul Brooks, *The House of Life: Rachel Carson at Work* (Boston: Houghton Mifflin Company, 1972), p. 319.
9. *The Record of the Orally Transmitted Teachings*, p. 200.
10. Ibid., p. 165.
11. Anthony Marsella, "Five New Year's Resolutions for the Promotion of Spiritual Perfection Through Humanistic Action," *Seikyo Shimbun*, January 1, 1995.
12. *Choose Life: A Dialogue*, p. 293.
13. Ibid., p. 301.

14. "Sela Sutta," *The Sutta-Nipata*, trans. H. Saddhatissa (London: Curzon Press, 1987), p. 65; "Maha Parinibbana Suttanta," *Dialogues of the Buddha*, Part II, trans. T. W. and C. A. F. Rhys Davids (London: Henry Frowde), pp. 79–81.

15. *The Writings of Nichiren Daishonin*, vol. I, p. 579.

16. Ibid., p. 402.

17. *The Record of the Orally Transmitted Teachings*, p. 115.

18. *All Men Are Brothers*, p. 49.

Index

multinational cooperation, 18, 40
mutual influences, 9–16
Mystic Law, devotion to the, 34

Nagasaki, Japan, bombing of, 50,
    54, 66
nallik, 123, 124
the nation, 17
national boundaries, 108
nationalism, 108, 144
National League of Cities, 128
national sovereignty, 136, 142–146
Native Americans. *See* American
    Indians
nature, 26–27, 61, 62. *See also* the
    environment
    connection to, 88–89
Nazis, 12, 19, 20, 92, 111
Nazism, 103
Needham, Massachusetts, 102
neighborhoods, 89
Neolithic Europe, 109
Neumann, Erich, *The Great Mother*,
    109
New Jersey, 5, 10, 26
New Jersey College of Women, 4
Nichiren, 8, 20, 137, 138, 141
    "On Establishing the Correct
        Teaching for the Peace of the
        Land," 145
Nichiren Buddhism, 34, 68, 137,
    138, 141, 145
Nitobe, Inazo, 35
nongovernmental organizations,
    35, 44, 82, 118–120, 127–129.
    See also peace movements;
    specific organizations
nonviolence, 49–55, 117, 122, 125,
    126
    nonviolence networks, 22
    nonviolence training, 70, 128

nonviolent resistance, 19–20,
    20
North America, 107. *See also specific*
    countries
Northern Europe, welfare systems
    of, 45
the North-South gap, 42, 43, 45,
    134, 136
Norway, 95, 101, 102
    cooperative spirit of, 17–22
    female leadership in, 77
    welfare society in, 18, 45
    during World War II, 19–20, 111
"Nuclear Arms: Threat to
    Humanity" exhibition, 22, 93
nuclear weapons, xiii–xiv, 93, 127–
    128. *See also* arms control;
    disarmament; weapons
    technology
nuns, 109
nurturing, 122–123

Obama, Barack, xi–xii
oceans, 127–128
Ogata, Sadako, 40
Okinawa, Japan, 54
Oksenberg, Michel, 135
Omori district, Tokyo, 10
"On Establishing the Correct
    Teaching for the Peace of the
    Land," 145
the One-Third World, 42, 45
optimism, 104
ordinary people, 109–113
Orthodox Christianity, 118
Oslo, Norway, 17–18
Oslo Accords, 19
Ottoman Turks, 138
outcomes, imagining real, 91–92
outer space, 127–128

About the Authors

ELISE M. BOULDING is Professor of Sociology Emerita of Dartmouth College, where she developed the nation's first peace studies program. She has served on the board of the United Nations University, the International Jury of the UNESCO Prize for Peace, and the Congressional Commission that led to the establishment by Congress of a U.S. Peace Institute. Her written works include *Cultures of Peace: The Hidden Side of History* (2000), *Abolishing War: Cultures and Institutions* (with Randall Forsberg, 1998), *The Future: Images and Processes* (with Kenneth Boulding, 1994), and *Building a Global Civic Culture: Education for an Interdependent World* (1990).

DAISAKU IKEDA is President of the Soka Gakkai International, a lay Buddhist organization with more than twelve million members worldwide. He has written and lectured widely on Buddhism, humanism, and global ethics. More than fifty of his dialogues have been published, including conversations with figures such as Mikhail Gorbachev, Hazel Henderson, Joseph Rotblat, Linus Pauling, and Arnold Toynbee. Dedicated to education promoting humanistic ideals, in 1971 President Ikeda founded Soka University in Tokyo and, in 2001, Soka University of America in Aliso Viejo, California.